I0063316

THE EXCEPTIONAL MIDDLE MANAGER

THE
EXCEPTIONAL

MIDDLE
MANAGER

HOW TO THINK SMARTER,
BUILD HIGH-PERFORMANCE TEAMS,
AND ADVANCE YOUR CAREER IN TODAY'S WORKPLACE

JEFF LYON

PUBLISHING

© 2023 Jeff Lyon
Published by J.L.Lyon, LLC

All rights reserved. No part of this book may be reproduced or used in any
manner without the prior written permission of the copyright owner, except for
the use of brief quotations in a book review.

To request permissions, contact the author: jeffllyon@outlook.com

Printed in the United States of America.
First paperback edition March 2023.

Cover and layout design by G Sharp Design, LLC.
www.gsharpmajor.com

ISBN: 979-8-9876280-0-3 (paperback)
ISBN: 979-8-9876280-1-0 (ebook)

Library of Congress Control Number: 2023901187

This book is dedicated to everyone I ever worked for or worked with, including all of my mentoring clients. It is because of the quality time I've spent with all of you that I have developed these insights to share with the rest of the managers and leaders who can benefit from this information in the future.

CONTENTS

INTRODUCTION

Upon opening this book, your first question might be, "Who exactly is a middle manager... am *I* a middle manager?" Well, we could debate the terminology for a while, but I'd rather refer to this excerpt from a 2021 Harvard Business Review article:

> *"They [middle managers] are the engine of the business, the cogs that make things work, the glue that keeps companies together. Especially as remote and hybrid work takes over — and the distance between employees increases — middle managers are more important than ever."* [1]

If that quote describes your role in your organization, and if you have levels of management above you, and other people, especially more junior managers or leaders reporting to you, then for purposes of this book, yes, you are a middle manager.

As any manager reading this knows, there is an endless supply of books on management, leadership, and self-actualization available to us at all times, both online and in bookstores. Managers buy these books because they are continuously striving to discover information and insights that will make them better managers, make their jobs easier, and improve their opportunity for career advancement. In my experience, most management books—while full of stimulating concepts, guidelines, models, and theories—don't really help much with the difficult, real-world challenges that middle managers confront every day. That's why I decided to write what I hope will serve as a valuable, practical guide on how to think smarter, build high-performance teams, and advance your career in today's workplace.

To be clear, I am not trying to launch a trendy new management model or executive coaching program in this book. In fact, this discussion isn't aimed at top executives at all. Instead, this book is intended to be a frank and honest communication between us middle managers, a discussion that should also be of value to first-line managers and other high performers who are headed for management.

At the time of this writing, we are approaching the end of the Covid pandemic era. These are chaotic times indeed. Business leaders worldwide are having to face a host of unprecedented challenges—"The Great Resignation," employees working from home, employees "quitting in place," corporate downsizing, supply chain shortages, growing concerns about inflation, and cultural and social changes of all kinds. The middle manager of today is expected to deal with all these issues, while continuing to successfully run the operations of their organization. These managers need expert, practical, and tactical advice—not abstract theories, idealistic models and checklists that don't fit the real world that they operate in every day. They need to know how to become an *Exceptional Middle Manager.*

So, what qualifies me to be your management trail guide? I've succeeded in a variety of management roles going back to the '80s. I rose to the level of Vice President of Retail Operations in the banking industry before crossing over to the tech sector in the early '90s, which ultimately led to a successful management career at Microsoft, followed by several years as a management consultant, coach, and mentor. Simply put, I spent a lot of years in the middle management trenches; I learned how to succeed in that space; I've taught others how to succeed, and now I'm hoping to share my insights and observations with a wider audience of managers.

The most significant periods in my career were my years at Bank of America, Pacific Bank, Attachmate, and Microsoft, followed by several years at Revel Consulting, Red Cloud Consulting, and The Simms Group. For the most part, those are the organizations and experiences I'll be referencing throughout the book.

Today, I'm semi-retired, looking back on a successful run of about 25 years in the tech industry preceded by about 15 years in the banking industry. I say semi-retired because I still do some mentoring and coaching engagements, mostly with middle managers in the tech sector. I truly love this mentoring work and will probably keep it up for as long as I can. As the old saying goes, "It's not work if you love doing it."

It is largely because of the positive feedback I receive from these mentoring discussions—and prior decades spent coaching the managers who reported to me—that I realized there are quite a few things I learned along the way that could help other people in their own career journeys. This book is my way of sharing these insights with a broader audience i.e., my attempt to reach more people than I ever could via my private mentoring and coaching practice.

Over the years, many managers, leaders, and other high achievers have reached out to me when they weren't sure what step to take next, what decision to make, what career path to choose, or simply what was the "right" thing to do. It dawned on me that many of the people I've worked with have been high achievers all of their lives, which often meant they were exceptional at following the rules, exceeding expectations, and receiving praise and rewards for their accomplishments. But high achievers often hit challenging points in their careers where there are difficult choices to be made, there are no clear rules, and there is no trustworthy support team to guide them. Years ago, when mentoring people in this type of situation, I started using the phrase "be your own agent," which essentially means that unless you have someone else looking out for your best interests every step of the way, you're going to have to perform that role yourself. And that means learning to think objectively about what's *truly* best for you, which is not necessarily what anyone else might want or expect you to do. Throughout this book, you will find advice on how you, as an exceptional middle manager, can be your own agent and achieve strategic advantage.

In the following pages, I will share the learnings, lessons, discoveries, and guiding principles that benefited me and the managers I supported and coached during *my* career, in the hope that I can help you navigate the challenges of *your* career.

One point I'd like to make right up front: the role of middle manager is particularly challenging… some might even say thankless. You are managing the core operations of your organization, and all too often you must do so while experiencing various pressures coming from both the levels above you and the people who report to you. We've all heard the adage "it's lonely at the top," and I'd amend that to say there's a certain amount of loneliness at every level of management. But if you've made it this far in your career, that hopefully means the positives have outweighed the negatives for you, and you're interested in progressing further on your management career path. Of course, sometimes you may find yourself struggling in a middle management or leadership role, unsure how to transform it from a negative to a positive experience. This book is intended to give you some of the answers you need.

You may notice that, at different points in the book, I'm fairly critical of certain types of executive managers. While we've probably all seen plenty to criticize among some of the senior execs we've worked for and read about, I want to emphasize that I have also had the pleasure of working under some very impressive top executives and I have considerable admiration for them. The ones who come to mind include Richard Cooley at Bank of America/Seafirst; John Dean, former CEO of Pacific First Bank; Kevin Johnson, former Microsoft exec and former CEO of Starbucks; Satya Nadella, the current CEO of Microsoft; Vikas Kamran, former CEO of Revel Consulting; Brett Alston, CEO of Red Cloud Consulting; Mike Simms, former CPO at Microsoft, and current CEO of the Simms Group; and of course, Bill Gates himself, who, while not always the best people manager I've ever seen, was always brilliant, a thought leader for the world, and perhaps the most generous person who ever lived.

So, let's get started…

Right from the outset, I'm going to assume that the person reading this book is—or soon will be—a manager and leader with a team to manage, people to lead, deliverables to deliver, budgets to adhere to, and goals to achieve—including personal career goals—with the need to carefully plan all of it. Let's focus on the planning part first …

PART 1

HOW MIDDLE MANAGERS CAN THINK SMARTER AND PLAN BETTER

CHAPTER 1
SETTING GOALS AND OBJECTIVES

Throughout my career, and in many different workplaces, I've seen group after group, especially those in "back-office" staff functions, (e.g. Finance, HR, Marketing, Procurement, Field Support, etc.) struggle to define their mission, goals, and objectives. There are often endless meetings, long discussions, and some level of confusion about what we're even talking about: mission vs. vision, strategies vs. goals, goals vs. objectives, etc. etc.

In my view, managers at all levels tend to seriously over-complicate the task of explaining their purpose and specifying what they want to achieve in the foreseeable future. All too often, the planning exercise becomes overly focused on messaging, i.e., slide-building and presentations, and not enough on the results they have to achieve in order to succeed.

Simply put, your strategy development should be focused on how to achieve success, not on how your presentation is going to impress some leader above you in the organization. Enlightened executives are far more interested in successful outcomes than in flashy presentations, and the ones who value form over substance tend to be gone in a couple of years.

Early in my career at Microsoft, as a participant in a special management development program, I received some invaluable coaching from a highly respected senior executive. The exec shared two principles with me that I've continued to employ and re-share over the years:

→ **Never publish more than 3-5 goals or priorities for your organization.** People can remember 3-5 things and they can align their efforts with a focus on achieving these top priorities. (When those are achieved, you can add 3-5 more.) If you create a whole lot more than that, nobody remembers what they all are, and you risk not achieving any of them.

→ **The role of a leader is to get out ahead of the team and "lay track,"** i.e., anticipate where the organization needs to go, prepare them to go there, and make sure that direction is reflected in strategies and goals. There are some risks associated with this analogy: if you get out too far ahead of your organization, you can lose connection with what's going on now, and others may see you as a hopeless visionary. Conversely, if you don't get out far enough ahead of the team and plan ahead, e.g., if you're overly involved in day-to-day operations, then you're at risk of the current situation overtaking you with problems and questions you are not prepared to respond to.

There should always be continuity in how you express your organization's mission, vision, strategies, and goals, from the top exec's goals all the way to the individual employee's. If you don't see that level of consistency across these elements in your organization—if individual goals don't really map back to the mission and vision that have been published for your overall organization—you should call "time out" and go back and figure out how you got out of sync.

High on the list of morale killers in an organization is recognizing that what you're actually working on every day bears little resemblance to what someone above you claims the organization is committed to. For example, if you worked for the mythical "ACME" company presented below, and your assigned goals don't appear to be related in any way to the sales of Model A, the testing of Model B, or the planning of Model C, you should have a discussion with whomever assigned your goals and find out why.

Here are some simple definitions of my own that might help you in differentiating between planning elements during your planning cycle:

		HYPOTHETICAL ACME EXAMPLE
MISSION	A statement of our purpose, our reason for being, the value we strive to deliver, sometimes constrained in scope e.g., by geography, business sector, etc. Keep it simple; keep it real; and don't over-reach into things you can't actually control.	*"Provide the highest quality, most technically advanced, safest and most reliable materials used in spacesuit construction worldwide."*
VISION	The end-state condition that we would love to achieve within a period of time, typically long term. Often an ideal that we know we may never fully achieve, but hopefully one that informs our decisions and helps us to prioritize.	*"By the end of the decade, every astronaut from every country will be wearing a suit made from ACME materials."*
STRATEGIES	Our best ideas for the activities and deliverables we should focus on in the upcoming period, in order to make progress toward the desired end-state.	*"This year we will focus on:* • *Increasing month-over-month sales of Model A.* • *Continuing to be a market leader by finalizing design and launching production of Model B by mid-year.* • *Achieving certification for the future Model C that will meet or exceed new government standards that go into effect in the year 20xx."*
OBJECTIVES	The specific outcomes and milestones we hope to achieve while executing on our strategies. Objectives can exist at the program level, and the project level, as well as the individual level. High quality objectives focus on *results* rather than *activities* (a strong guiding principle that I will repeat several times in the pages ahead) *Note: I regard objectives and goals to be essentially the same thing.*	*"Sales of Model A will reach $x/mo by end of Q2, $y/mo by end of Q3, $z/mo by end of Q4."* *"Rip-stop testing for Model B will achieve no more than x defects per thousand by mid-year."* *"Prototype for Model C will be approved for production by end of Q3."*

Here are some additional guidelines that can help you to develop your plan based on meaningful, applicable, and achievable goals:

→ Don't sign up for something you actually can't control. Signing up for someone else's goals—like sales goals when you're not even in sales, or customer satisfaction goals when you never have any customer contact— might feel admirable and collaborative in the moment but could lead to your own failure when that other group you're sharing with doesn't meet *their* goals.

→ Don't make emotional, idealistic statements or set unrealistic goals, e.g., using terms like "best in class," "world class," "perfect every time," "zero defects." Those aren't goals; they're vague, undefined and/or unattainable aspirations.

→ Avoid impressive-sounding but unmeasurable verbs like "own," "lead," "drive," "support," "partner" and "collaborate," that don't actually have a specific, agreed-upon meaning. You don't want to end up in a performance review debating whether you "drove" hard enough or delivered enough units of collaboration during the review period.

→ The goal statement is not a job description; it is a statement of the tangible value each person is expected to deliver during a specified period of time (all goals should have end-dates). Again, it's critically important to focus on *deliverables* rather than *activi-*

ties. Make it clear what results are expected rather than focusing on how employees are spending time. Focus on *nouns* instead of *verbs*.

➜ Think critically about the justification for each goal, bearing in mind that the only valid justification is that it contributes to our ability to deliver the results we're responsible for. Goals are not the place to make broad policy statements or vision statements. Goals are about achieving specific, observable, measurable outcomes at specific points in time. Be very careful about signing up for any goals that you aren't certain will lead to the results that you're personally responsible for.

➜ Beware of what I call a "pattern-match,": committing to a goal not because we're certain there is a clear benefit, but mostly because some other organization does it. Or, because someone up the line thinks the "optics" would be good if we all sign up for something that seems important to someone even further up the line. Or simply because we've always signed up for it in the past. Don't be afraid to speak up when a goal that someone is requesting doesn't really relate to what you are responsible for. I will go into more depth on the concept of "pattern-match" decision-making in the next section.

➜ If you'd like to experience more success in the future than you've had in the past, a good place to start is in renegotiating your goals to define a clear and indisputable path to increased recognition and reward.

As I called out in the Introduction, I like to use the term "be your own agent" (unless you actually have an agent). Here's an example of how your agent might approach the people who approve your goals, so don't be afraid to have a discussion with your manager that goes something like this:

> *"This is how I'd like to be viewed at the end of the review period. What results do you need to see this year that will convince you I've achieved my objectives and deserve to be rewarded accordingly?"*

If your manager doesn't have a clue how to answer that question, see the section below on making your next career move.

In short, when it comes to mission, vision, strategies, and goals, make it clear, and make it real. Your employees will love you for it.

It's True: if You Can't Measure It, You Can't Manage It

If a goal doesn't meet the definition of **SMART**—**S**pecific, **M**easurable, **A**chievable, **R**elevant, and **T**ime-Based—then it's not really a goal at all.[2]

Here are a couple of time-worn but still meaningful old sayings that relate to this point:

"A goal without a plan is just a wish."[3]

"If you don't know where you're going, any road will get you there."[4]

We've talked above about making it real, and that encompasses the **S**pecific **A**chievable and **R**elevant dimensions of the SMART model. But it's in making it **M**easurable and **T**ime-Based that a lot of managers fall down. We don't have the time or space here to go into a deep discussion of metrics, analytics, business intelligence, etc. but here's a simple guideline that might help you:

A strong goal should answer the questions: "What?," "How much?," and "By when?"

If you can't answer any of those questions, you should determine why. Is it because the data you need to measure progress doesn't exist? Or, because there's really no agreement on what it is we're trying to accomplish or when we need it done? Or, is it because the statement you're looking at isn't really a goal at all?

This is where metrics and reporting come in. First, it's important to point out that reporting is absolutely essential to your ability to know whether you're making progress toward the goals that you set for yourself and your team. One of the banking execs I worked for put it best:

"Inspect what you expect."

But too often we find ourselves tracking a whole bunch of numbers that don't accurately measure progress on the variables we care about most. Especially in the era of big data, it's critical to recognize that there's a huge gap between the universe of all the data that you have access to and could be monitoring on a regular basis, vs. the handful of key success indicators that accurately reflect progress toward the outcomes you are responsible for. Put more simply, just because you *can* monitor something, doesn't mean you *should*.

In this context, the concept of *causation* is especially important. Can you isolate the independent variable from the dependent variables? Are you able to verify a direct cause-and-effect relationship vs. a coincidence where things seem to vary at the same time but it's not clear whether one is causing the other or whether something else is the real driver? For example, I see countless customer reviews on Amazon where the customer is giving the product a low rating because the package didn't arrive on time. So, where is the problem that needs to be solved—in manufacturing, packaging, or delivery? If you don't identify the real cause of customer dissatisfaction, you risk spending cycles trying to solve the wrong problem.

We could go into great depth here, but here's a simple way to think about how to address the challenge: the first priority is to make sure you are absolutely clear about the outcomes you are expected to deliver, whether it's dollars, widgets, lines of code, service levels, regulatory compliance, or whatever... and remember:

Focus on nouns, not verbs; outcomes, not activities.

Next, work hard to isolate the measures that best provide evidence of achievement in that area and then negotiate agreed-upon goals based on those measures. Once you've locked down the goals, regularly gather data on those measures, analyze that data, and determine what action, if any, should be taken to meet or exceed your goals. When you need to report progress to someone above you in the management chain, it should be in terms of the same agreed-upon measures you use to monitor your team's progress.

Now, with that basic approach as background, please take a moment to think about the metrics and management information that you are responsible for reporting today, and ask yourself: "Do I report this information because it's important to me and my ability to manage my business... or only because someone else up the line asked for it and we have no choice but to comply?" As a management consultant, I have often been troubled to see how much work my clients are putting into developing metrics, business intelligence, and reporting from which they get no personal value. This is so prevalent in some work cultures that it doesn't even occur to middle managers that any report they're developing ought to have some value at their own level. Instead, reports are seen as administrative overhead, as a tax you must pay in order to satisfy the managers above you. In the more severe cases, I've seen this kind of pass-through reporting go through multiple levels that don't extract any value from the reports, yet they continue to require them because they believe that someone even higher up the organization cares about some metric that the rest of us don't value.

There are two things wrong with this scenario. First, as the title of this section stated, if you can't measure it, you can't manage it. It's also true that even when you can measure it, data is of limited value if the results have little relevance for your organization. If the data you are capturing and reporting is meaningful only to someone other than you, then you should spend some serious time thinking about the evidence you actually need in order to assess the performance of your team, and each individual within it. And then you should encourage everyone up the line to focus on the same data that you use to run your business.

Secondly, if some level of management above you wants to see metrics that you don't feel accurately reflect your business, then you and that person are out of sync. One of you likely needs to change your perspective on what you're accountable for and how best to monitor performance.

As a final point on the topic of reporting, I've seen far too many cases where far too many people are spending far too many hours trying to cobble together a report that some exec has asked for without understanding the impact of their request. In other words, the exec does not know that the requested data is not readily available, or is not available in the format requested, and that it's going to take a lot of work to create a reasonable facsimile. It has often occurred to me that if the exec understood the burden they've created, along with why that data is not readily available, and why you don't regard that data as critical, and how many wasted hours it is going to take to create it, they might readily say, "Oh, don't bother with all of that, just show me what you think addresses my concern." Bottom line: if you simply clarify what the exec is concerned about, you can make a better decision about how to assemble available data to address that concern or how to explain that the necessary data isn't actually available.

An enlightened exec doesn't really want to waste your time and reduce your productivity. Sometimes the challenge has more to do with the layers of management between you and that exec. That is, people are afraid to simply explain that the requested report is not readily available and is not the best solution, and then to counter-offer a better, cost-effective alternative that meets everyone's needs. Believe me, I know how difficult it is, but a little push-back can sometimes help to avoid a costly waste of time and effort. This is one way you can *achieve strategic advantage* in the workplace. Another way, avoiding faulty pattern-match thinking, is covered in the next chapter.

CHAPTER 2
BEWARE OF FAULTY PATTERN-MATCH THINKING

B efore we begin this discussion of what I'm calling a "pattern-match," it's important to first recognize the importance of pattern-recognition in the way that humans learn, perceive the world, and make decisions. So, I hope you don't mind if we touch briefly on the academic side of this topic.

First, we can probably all agree that it's human nature to look for and recognize patterns in the things we see, hear, feel and otherwise experience. In fact, pattern-recognition is a key capability that we utilize when we're learning and recalling information about the world around us. We learn at a very young age to avoid things that are too hot, too cold, too sharp, etc. Simply put, pattern-recognition is critical to the survival of our, and all other species.

Ray Kurzweil, a leading expert on how the human brain works—and on how artificial intelligence is going to have to work in the future in order to simulate a human brain—says pattern-recognition is one of the most fundamental and important elements of human cognition. Our memory is largely based on our brains' pattern-recognition abilities. By creating an orderly sequential pattern, we exploit our brains' natural memory storage process to help us memorize things.[5]

It's not hard to recognize that much of what you have learned—about language, numbers, science, nature, people, music and everything else—has to a great degree been made possible by your ability to see and remember the patterns and relationships that exist in each of those areas. In primitive times, our ability to remember which animals were predators vs. prey, which plants were edible vs. poison, or which tribes were friends vs. enemies, was critical to our ability to survive and prosper.

So, what does all of that have to do with being an exceptional middle manager? The point I want to make here is that people often tend to have an unwarranted level of confidence in their own pattern-recognition capabilities... sometimes to the extent that they see a pattern where no pattern actually exists.

Here's a simple example: many people believe there are patterns relating to luck or fate, especially when they're playing a game or gambling. One of the key reasons that some gamblers get in over their heads and lose more money than they expected to is because they believed their "luck was going to change"… and it didn't, or because they believed it wasn't going to change… and it did.

The simplest illustration of this human trait is a coin toss. Suppose, for example, that someone is flipping a coin and it's your job to guess the outcome each time. Let's assume that the coin has come up heads several times in a row. Whether you've guessed right or wrong each time, after seeing several heads in a row, many people might have an intuitive, confident sense that there is a pattern here and that the odds of getting tails is increasing, i.e., their luck is going to change, so they guess tails. In reality, there is the exactly the same 50/50 probability that the coin is going to come up heads or tails each time. Whatever it was last time has no bearing on what it's going to be next time. This is a simple example of faulty pattern-recognition, assuming and expecting a pattern where a pattern doesn't really exist. When you find yourself in situations like this, it might be useful to stop for a moment and think critically about what forces would have to exist in the universe to control the pattern you thought you were observing, be it a coin toss, a slot machine, or a lottery ticket. Luck can't change if luck has nothing to do with what's going on in the first place.

The reason I've raised this topic of human pattern-recognition here is that I want to point out how our often-unconscious faith in this powerful cognitive capability can sometimes work to our disadvantage when making decisions in a business environment.

To be sure, pattern-recognition is an invaluable tool in problem solving when it's applied correctly, for example when you perceive that a problem you need to solve today is the same as a problem you solved in the past, such that the same solution should work again this time. This is an efficient and valuable application of the experience and wisdom you've accumulated to date. In fact, this is a major reason why we value experience in the workplace. However, the risk occurs when you incorrectly assume there's a pattern-match and there actually isn't. There are several different pattern-match scenarios that I'd like to discuss.

Scenario 1: Right Problem/Wrong Solution

This scenario is often associated with the manager who consistently employs a personal bias, insisting on the same solution for every problem. To paraphrase Abraham Maslow and others, "If the only tool you have is a hammer, it is tempting to treat everything as if it were a nail."[6] I can't help but think of the father in the film "My Big Fat Greek Wedding" who insisted that every problem could be solved with Windex.

You will see this phenomenon in all aspects of life, including business, politics, sports, parenting, and more. Some people think you can solve all problems with money, or charm, or deception, or whatever their tool of choice is. One powerful example of this is the parent who, in times of challenge, tends to fall back on the methods that their own parents used. This is so common it's almost unconscious, but if you think about it critically, is the approach your parents used really the best approach available… or just the one you're most familiar with?

Just to provoke a little creative thinking, I sometimes like to pose this thought for consideration: if you really love the way you turned out, then by all means, follow the same parenting approach your parents employed. However, if there are things about yourself that you wish were different, perhaps you should consider a different approach than your parents used. The principle here can be applied to all types of management scenarios too, often illuminated by the question "And how did that turn out for you?"

Some managers think you should address all problems with authority, bullying, and dominance, while others might lean toward kindness, empathy, and consensus-building. As we'll discuss later in the section on High-Performance Teams, there is no one "right way," and you should adjust your management approach to align to the situation you are dealing with in the moment.

Another example of a faulty pattern-match is when you don't actually have a preferred solution for a common problem, so you copy what someone else has done, perhaps because you think they are smarter or more experienced than you. In other words, you match someone else's pattern. I recall a moment years ago when I was in a meeting with the president of the bank I worked for. We were on a high-level floor in a downtown office building, and he was literally looking out the window, across the downtown area at the headquarters building of a top competitor in that market. He said to our group, "Their cost as a percent of revenue is way better than ours; we need to figure out how they're doing it and do the same thing here." In that instance, his attempt to pattern-match on that other company didn't make sense; they were unlike our company in many ways—size, product mix, etc.—and trying to emulate them was not going to work. In fairness though, I have to acknowledge another scenario where this same president recognized that in order to move in the direction we wanted to go, we were going to have to develop a team of highly skilled "personal bankers" who were "just as good as the agents at Merrill Lynch." So, he hired the guy that trained the people at Merrill Lynch, and he succeeded in launching a highly successful personal banker program. This was an example of smart pattern-matching, getting the problem and the solution right.

Before we leave the category of right problem/wrong solution, it's also worth pointing out that in all scenarios having to do with problems and solutions, there is frequently personal bias that leads people to avoid a perfectly good solution, simply because they didn't like it in the past. This too is a powerful trait in human nature. When something caused pain or difficulty in the past, or when it was associated with someone we don't like or respect, we tend to avoid it in the future. For example, sometimes a new leader who didn't respect the previous leader feels compelled to replace the inherited management team with their "own people," even when the current team has been doing a great job. It is always worth considering whether you are rejecting a perfectly good solution for no good reason.

Scenario 2: Wrong Problem/Wrong Solution

Sometimes the faulty pattern-match happens because we don't take sufficient time to fully understand the problem we're looking at in the current situation. On the surface, it looks familiar, so we use the same solution we usually employ for this type of problem and then we may be confused when this time the problem isn't resolved.

Here's an example: during my consulting career, I worked closely with a group that specialized in providing data protection support to other groups. This group had a special challenge trying to figure out which metrics they should use to measure their own impact. Think about it: if your role is to help other groups avoid data breaches, how do you measure your own effectiveness? How do you measure the non-event? And how do you determine whether it was your advice and guidance, or the client's action or inaction that was responsible for the outcome?

Creating meaningful metrics, and associated goals and objectives in this workspace was no easy task. The manager desperately needed metrics and advanced business intelligence and scorecards to deliver to senior management but the team was struggling to produce meaningful measures and acceptable reports. One person after another would join this fast-growing group, look at this metrics problem and say, "I know what to do." The recurring pattern-match error in this instance involved each person thinking, "We had good metrics and reporting in my last department; I'll just emulate what they did and solve this problem for my new group." Some even signed up to deliver the long-awaited solution within a few days or weeks.

In reality, several years went by without a good solution. The reason? The problem-solvers continued to make the error of assuming that the problem in this space was the same as the problem that was already solved in some other space they were familiar with. In this instance, they assumed the challenge was one of how to *report* metrics, when in fact it was a different and very challenging problem of how to *define* meaningful metrics in a scenario where ownership and accountability were blurry, and where success was actually measured in terms of the absence of something. It was a classic case of a solution looking for a problem and getting it wrong.

Over time, this group did figure out a solution that was acceptable to their management. But it took several years of faulty pattern-matching before they got it right.

Scenario 3: There Is No Problem, So Any Solution Is Wrong

In this scenario, the antidote to making faulty pattern-matches is to consistently ask this question...

"What problem does it solve?"

If you cannot answer this question—if you cannot identify a problem that is truly worth solving—then you may be on the verge of wasting time, effort, and money on something that does not help you to achieve your business goals.

A great example of this is when some leader decides that we have to do something a certain way because some other group, division, or company does it that way and we think we might look bad if we don't do it too. Sometimes this perspective is all based on someone thinking the "optics" are a risk… even when they have no data or proof that optics are even relevant in the current situation.

Sometimes we may match the pattern of what we think someone above us in the organization is looking for, not because it's the best solution to a legitimate problem, but because we're trying to impress—or not disappoint—someone who could judge us badly.

I recall a situation where a very senior executive cared a great deal about how we designed our slide presentations. It wasn't as much about the content as it was about the graphic elements used—fonts, shapes, colors, special effects, etc. Many people in many departments worked hard to adopt the pre-scribed graphic standards and then to re-adopt new standards, typically as the company's customer-facing advertising graphic style changed, and communications specialists struggled to emulate it for internal presentations. Endless hours and millions of dollars were expended in trying to adhere to these standards. But at the end of the day, they had little to do with how well our managers managed or were able to discuss the problems and solutions within the portion of the business they were responsible for. In essence, there was no problem here that needed to be solved, but we expended tons of resources solving it anyway, simply due to a personal preference. It's worth noting that a very successful big tech competitor across town actually prohibited the use of PowerPoint presentations in business meetings, and they have succeeded very well without incurring the burden of endless tuning of slideware.

There are countless examples to be found in this category. Another one that I encountered recently related to a company that was working to implement employee bonus programs. Someone on the team proposed copying the bonus model from their old company. The discussion had proceeded quite a way down the road before someone asked, "Why do we need a bonus program? Is it because we cannot attract and retain the people we want without one, or is it because everybody else seems to have one, our old companies had one, and we believe we need to match them, even when we have no data to support that commitment?"

Again, when your organization is about to spend precious dollars and hours creating a solution, it's smart to first ask the question: "What problem does it solve?"

Scenario 4: There Is a Problem, but I Can't See a Pattern

A major reason that managers and organizations fail, sometimes on a colossal level, is because they cannot clearly see when a new pattern is emerging that requires their attention. There are examples all around us of once-dominant companies, or technologies, or beliefs that could not adapt fast enough to changing realities and ultimately could no longer compete and survive.

Over years in the tech industry, I saw numerous once-successful companies, divisions, teams, or work groups struggle to understand why they were no longer performing at the high level they enjoyed in the past, especially if they had experienced a highly successful start-up phase. Often, people who had ridden an initial wave of success were anxious to reclaim the glory of their earlier years. They failed to recognize that the world had moved on and that new, disruptive patterns were emerging. Too often, management is convinced that "getting back to our roots," or "getting back to basics," or "getting back to what got us here in the first place" is the solution. They look backwards to patterns that are no longer relevant, rather than looking forward and discovering the new patterns that are emerging today.

Sometimes this failure to see what's right in front of you is an example of what I call "management by wishful thinking"—that is, a conscious or unconscious attempt to avoid the complexity of something you do not comprehend and replace it instead with something simpler that you are more comfortable with (see more on the topic of management by wishful thinking in Chapter 4).

Put another way...

Those who consistently over-simplify reality are inclined to fail in the real world.

Along the way, I've concluded that the best leaders are the ones who are willing to embrace complexity, no matter how difficult, and wrestle it into submission.

At the time of this writing, we are slowly and painfully learning about the impact of pandemics on our professional and personal lives, and we can see some of the same elements of faulty pattern-matching taking place. When something is novel and unprecedented and we simply don't see the magnitude of what's coming, it may be reasonable at first to say, "I can't imagine…" (because I don't see the pattern). In the early days of the Covid-19 pandemic, many people were unable to imagine the ultimate impact of the coronavirus. They assumed there was no way it could go on for longer than a few weeks, because 1, they'd never seen a virus do that before (no pattern-match), and 2, they simply couldn't imagine a world in which businesses, schools, and other venues could be closed and people would wear masks for months on end. Even in the face of clear facts, people could not perceive or envision the emerging pattern, and many therefore had a hard time believing and adapting. The ultimate cost of this failure to see and respond effectively to the pattern, in terms of business and personal financial losses and health-related issues experienced around the world, is immeasurable.

The Good News: Technology to the Rescue

Kurzweil points out that while there is an impressive capacity for storing information in the human neocortex, it is nevertheless limited. We will overcome that limitation in the future by expanding our brains into the cloud. In other words, we will use technology—especially artificial intelligence technology—to help us better detect emerging patterns and match the right solutions to the patterns we're observing.

Kurzweil thinks of technology as an "expander" of the considerable capabilities we already possess in the human brain. He says, "The amount of neocortex we have is what enables us to operate at a higher level relative to other animals. When we expand again via technology to the cloud there will be huge increase in our capabilities."[7]

Hopefully by now you understand how critical it is to set high quality goals and objectives, ideally based on an accurate assessment of problems and potential solutions (i.e., based on a good pattern-match). If you successfully employ the principles cited above, you will achieve a strategic advantage, and others will see you as a thought leader and a candidate for future advancement.

Of course, you can have a great plan, great vision, and great strategies, but if you don't have a team of talented people with the right skills and motivation to deliver on your strategies, then you're at risk of failing anyway. So, let's spend some time talking about how to hire, develop, reward, and retain the people you need.

PART 2

HOW TO BUILD HIGH-PERFORMANCE TEAMS IN THE MODERN WORKPLACE

CHAPTER 3

HIRING: IT'S YOUR HIGHEST PRIORITY

If you come away from this chapter understanding only one thing, let it be this:

Hiring is the most important job that people managers do.

Unfortunately, it's often also one of the top things that busy managers don't do well.

In the relatively rare instance when you're launching a new organization with newly created positions to fill, you might enjoy the luxury of having adequate time and inducements to source all the talent you need. But more often, an open position occurs as an unplanned, unexpected interruption that no one has time for, and as a result, the task of filling that position may not compete well for resources and attention.

In my view, you will achieve a strategic advantage by understanding that filling an open position must be viewed as "Job 1". Here's why:

→ At all times, you need the most talent you can possibly get in each position on your team. Anything less is to some degree a compromise, a shortfall between what could be vs. what is.

→ Most of an organization's work is done by the employees, not the manager(s). Let me state that again: employees, not managers, do most of the work. If your organization is designed and staffed correctly—i.e., if you previously had the right number and quality of resources to get the job done well—then any reduction in resources is a problem that you need to solve ASAP.

→ Many managers fail to focus sufficient attention on hiring because, in the midst of all the urgent pressures and external demands competing for a manager's attention, hiring might seem like one thing that can be postponed for a little while; however...

→ An unfilled position on your team creates a burden on your organization, in addition to the other organizations and people—including customers—who depend on you. When you allow a position to remain open, other team members often have to take up the slack and cover for the vacant position, or else the work simply may not get done at all. The smaller your team, the bigger the negative impact of an unfilled position and, unfortunately, the harder it might be to find the bandwidth to focus on it. But you must.

→ As the work backlog increases and your team members feel the burden of covering somebody else's work, deadlines and deliverables can be missed and morale can be impacted, resulting in an increased risk of even more turnover. In other words, your failure to fill an open position quickly and effectively can result in you having more open positions to fill. You need to avoid that slippery slope.

→ In some scenarios, if a position remains unfilled for a long time, budget-minded people elsewhere in your organization might conclude that you seem to be doing fine with current resources, and they could take that unfilled position away from you. They may regard it as a cost reduction win, while you have now allowed a temporary burden on your team to become permanent. All that because you didn't make filling that position a top priority.

Years ago, I read in some trendy business book that managers will end up regretting two out of three of the hiring decisions they make. That seems a little excessive to me. On the other hand, I can't think of any manager I've ever worked with who was totally happy with every hiring decision they've made and who wouldn't love to upgrade some of the talent on their current team. Just being honest here.

Why do managers end up disappointed in so many of their hiring decisions? In some instances, the hiring manager may have thought they had found a worthy candidate but simply hadn't taken the time to thoroughly evaluate the candidate before hiring them. In other cases, the manager may have been unsure of the hiring decision right from the outset but felt compelled to hire a person anyway, possibly due to time constraints, an apparent lack of available options, pressure from someone sponsoring that candidate, or just a need to get *someone*—anyone—into the role .

I've seen other situations—too many actually—where the hiring manager was initially very happy with the hiring decision, believing they had brought someone onboard who was really going to make a difference… only to conclude months, or even years, later that they had made a mistake and never should have hired that person in the first place.

One area where I think many of us can be more effective in our hiring is around making sure that the candidate really does possess the skills that we think they do. This sounds obvious, but I've seen numerous hiring decisions based on the words and impressions presented in a well-crafted resume, a third-party referral, or an impressive interview, rather than on real evidence of what the candidate can actually *do*.

Sometimes hiring managers are so busy, we don't take the time to verify the claims made in resumes and interviews. How many of us have failed to follow up with a candidate's previous employers—even those within our own organizations—in order to find out whether the candidate is really as strong as they claim to be?

When I'm looking at a resume with the obligatory list of impressive "accomplishments," I like to consider this question:

Did the candidate actually *make these things happen*, or were they *just there when it happened?*

If you don't know the answer to that question, dig deeper.

Sometimes during the hiring process, we feel like we've done our due diligence, and the candidate has presented themselves well, but there's this nagging feeling that something seems to be missing. (Sound familiar?) Sometimes we wish we had asked another question, clarified a response, or gotten more third-party input on the candidate. But the clock is ticking; the candidate is waiting for a response, and maybe it feels like the only option is to just go for it.

Years ago, a seasoned exec gave me some advice that I never forgot: hiring is a critical responsibility, and the outcome will have huge impact on you, on your team, and on the person hired. You should take whatever steps are necessary, including meeting with the candidate as many times as you need to, or asking for a sample of the candidate's previous work, or having more members of your team (including stakeholders who will have to work closely with the candidate) assess the candidate and give you feedback in order to ensure that it's going to be a good hire.

Simply put, there's no law that says you must interview someone only once or that you owe them a final response within X hours of the first interview. Don't waste valuable time, but also don't hesitate to ask for whatever you need to make the best decision you can make. You owe this to the rest of your team and to yourself.

Regarding the Hiring of Managers

When I was leading a large customer support organization in a rapidly growing tech company, there was always a need for more first-level managers. This resulted in a lot of applications from existing employees who wanted to take their first crack at being a manager. Sometimes it was because they really wanted to manage, but all too often it was because they felt the only career path available to them was to move into management.

Early on, I noticed that some of them were obviously uncomfortable pursuing the management option. I learned to ask this thought-provoking question:

"Do you *need* to lead?"

This question is often unexpected, and it will typically reveal some important information that will help both you and the candidate to make better decisions than you might have otherwise.

I was working in the tech sector when I posed this question, so I was often talking to someone who was proud of their deep technical skills and conflicted about moving into a less technical career path. Our internal candidates tended to fall into two categories:

→ The technically-oriented person who was applying for a management role because they felt it was the only available career path. This person would often respond to the question with something like, "No, I don't *need* to lead, and I'd be happy to stay in a technical, individual contributor role. I just thought it might be important to show my interest in advancement. But please feel free to play me where I can add the most value."

→ However, on occasion there was another type of candidate who gave a different response like: "That's an interesting question. I love technology, but yes, I think I *do* need to lead in order to be happy in my career." This person typically had a history of being a natural leader—in their school, family, church, among their friends, team members, coworkers, etc.—and they were ready to perform a leadership role for the remainder of their career.

In my experience, it has been the people in the second category, the natural leaders, who have gone on to achieve the most success as managers.

As an interesting footnote to this "need to lead" trait: one time I was having an exit interview with the CEO of a bank I worked for. Our company had been acquired by another bank and we had both chosen to take a generous severance package rather than joining the acquiring bank. I asked him what he was thinking of doing next, and he responded, "You know, once you've been a CEO, you pretty much need to be a CEO for the rest of your career... so I'm only looking at CEO openings." I found that to be a fascinating insight that I carried with me ever since. Top execs *need* to be top execs. Don't ever forget it.

CHAPTER 4
HOW TO BUILD AND MAINTAIN HIGH-PERFORMANCE TEAMS

O ver all the years I have been in business, an endless succession of books and training models have been devoted to the topic of getting the most out of your team members. I wouldn't doubt that you too may have spent a small fortune sending your team—and yourself—to a variety of seminars and training events, hoping to improve performance across your organization. Many of us have been inspired by such learning, and sometimes our outcomes have improved as a result.

On the other hand, many of us are all too familiar with situations where no matter how much training was provided, how many advanced models were adopted, how many inspiring speeches were delivered, or how many rewards and incentives were distributed, we still didn't really achieve our vision and live up to the expectations we had set.

As I've stated before, the aim of this book is not to set forth a comprehensive new model of management. Instead, this is the place where I would like to deliver some simple, easily-remembered principles that I have found to be powerful and valuable for me, and for the managers I have coached and mentored.

The Best "Management Style"? It Depends…

Too often, people expect to learn something meaningful by asking, "What is your leadership style?", as if there is a short list of acceptable styles to choose from. They seem to believe it's as simple a question as "Where do you buy your clothes?," implying that how you answer that question will tell them all they need to know about you.

One point about management style before we go any further: when you are a manager in a hierarchical organization structure, by definition you have more authority than the people who report to you. The effective leader recognizes that they have a critical responsibility to exercise that authority in an honest, fair, respectful, supportive manner. We are not going to spend a lot of time discussing personal beliefs in this book, so hear this well: if you believe that you are superior to anyone else in your workplace purely based on title, race, gender, religion, country of origin, color of skin, sexual orientation, or any other attribute that is not explicitly related to skill and performance, you are simply wrong, and you risk failing in your career unless and until you get to work on discovering why you are wrong and then proceed to change your beliefs and behavior as needed. If you disagree with that statement, then this book will be of limited value to you. Let's move on…

For me, management style is actually a fuzzy concept and is likely more aligned to what kind of a person you are than to what kind of methodology you subscribe to. Having said that, as I have observed at least hundreds of managers applying their personal management approaches on a day-to-day basis, I've been consistently surprised at how many of them attempt to apply the same approach to every situation and to every employee, even when they are not getting the outcomes they want. To paraphrase another old saying:

> **Ineffective management is what you get when you apply the same approach over and over—and expect a different outcome.**

Of all the people-management models I've encountered over decades of management, I continue to think that one of the earliest I came across has held up as the most valid and useful. I'm not going to go so far as to endorse all the popular concepts, books, and courses developed by Ken Blanchard and Paul Hersey over the years, but when these two guys landed on their Situational Leadership model, I think they nailed it.[8]

During my years as a management consultant, I often found myself suggesting that the one-size-fits-all approach, or "style," a manager was using with a specific employee could not succeed because that employee was not at a level of development where they could understand and respond effectively to the guidance they were getting. After making this point repeatedly, it dawned on me that I was employing a concept I had learned and embraced long ago: "Situational Leadership." I started to recommend that time-tested training for many of my middle management clients, and I think many have benefited from it.

Like most management training models, Situational Leadership is deceptively simple in concept, but for complicated reasons it appears to be more difficult to practice than many people expect. The concept in a nutshell is that an exceptional middle manager knows they need to employ a different management "style" with each employee, based on each employee's development level. Rookies need more gentle guidance and oversight; high performing veterans can be given a lot of autonomy because you trust them to make good decisions and deliver quality results. Even as I'm writing these statements, this situational approach appears to be so obvious that it seems logical to assume every middle manager knows and practices this method. And yet, they don't.

One thing that employees often don't realize is that managers, all the way up to the tops execs, are not always sure of *themselves*, and often may not know with certainty what to do next. When you see a manager employing the same style—be it authoritarian, or more nurturing and col-laborative—over and over again, even when it's clearly not working, you may just be observing a key feature of human nature. We are habitual creatures, and we tend to stay with something that's familiar, especially if it seemed to work well at some point in the past.

Perhaps you can't blame a manager for assuming that whatever approach got them to where they are today is destined to bring them more success in the future. Later in the book we'll talk about the Peter Principle, another timeless gem; but for now suffice it to say that the most effective managers and leaders are the ones who repeatedly assess the current situation and adapt their approach—their "management style"—to be the most effective option in the moment.

Rather than go deeper into the tenets of Situational Leadership here, I will simply recommend that if you haven't had that training thus far in your career, you should pursue it now. You can start learning about it at https://situational.com.

Value Initiative Above All Other Attributes

When it comes to what kinds of talent and skill you need on your bench in order to succeed, over many years of observing the relative contributions of different kinds of players, I have come to value *initiative* over all other attributes.

By initiative, I don't just mean someone who merely works hard, or is driven to advance. (Don't confuse ambition with initiative.) Rather, I'm thinking of the person who will step up, volunteer, and take charge again and again regardless of whether there's an immediate payback for doing so.

Unfortunately, initiative is a trait that is often difficult to detect when you first meet a potential future employee. You can see the credentials they've earned, the accomplishments they've achieved, and the job titles they've had. Initiative, however, is an inner quality that all candidates profess to have, but too few employees actually exhibit in the workplace.

It's an unavoidable fact that many people often don't want to take on additional responsibility unless it benefits them personally in some way. And sometimes you can't blame them. After all, if we're all supposed to be laser-focused on achieving our personal objectives, doesn't it make sense to keep your head down, hit your goals, avoid risk, and reap the rewards? And isn't this especially true if you're being graded on a curve, i.e., stack-ranked against your teammates?

To be sure, that me-first approach works well for some people. In fact, for some it has worked extremely well over a succession of roles in their career. But these are not typically the people who are solving the big problems and showing us how to get to the next level.

The exceptional individual is the one who says, "I'll do it because it needs to be done," or "I'll do it because it will benefit the most people," or "I think I see a solution to this problem and I want to work on it." That is the essence of true initiative, and the more people like this you have on your team, the closer you will be to having a high-performance team that is capable of producing great outcomes.

The Art of Delegation (Don't Make It Personal)

I used the term "art" here somewhat facetiously. This is because I often encounter middle managers who are seriously confused about when, or how much, or to whom they should delegate. They often assume that there must be a simple answer to those questions, a simple technique they can quickly apply and then move on.

I think that where many managers get confused about delegation is that they tend to think about it only when it's personal—when it's about something they are personally doing and are wondering whether, how, and when they should transfer that task to someone else. In other words, managers tend to think about delegation most when they are personally feeling overloaded with work.

And, believe me, I've been there. At one time in my career, I was working very long hours, including nights and weekends. I had a large team—including several managers—reporting to me, but for a variety of reasons, I had decided that I needed to do a disproportionate amount of the work myself. I vividly remember sitting in my office one Sunday afternoon and thinking, "I am the only person in this building today; everyone else is out there enjoying their weekend. I've got a family waiting for me to get home. What's wrong with this picture?" Clearly, I had a delegation problem. But, as stated above, I was thinking about that problem more on a personal level than on an organizational level.

What I've learned since then, and what you may find enlightening now, is that it's important to take the time to think beyond your own personal workload and focus more broadly on how work is distributed across your team. It's essential to recognize that in a multi-person workgroup, the work has presumably *already* been delegated. Assuming that each person on your team has something to do every day then, by definition, delegation has occurred. Delegation is a built-in feature of organizational design, wherein the overall group is responsible for a set of deliverables, and each member of the group has been delegated some level of responsibility for a subset of those deliverables.

My perspective today is that delegation should not be viewed as a mysterious art at all, but rather as a well-planned, rational distribution of responsibilities. I think much of the uncertainty we experience regarding delegation can be attributed to the possibility that right from the beginning, we didn't set clear goals—with clear accountability for specific deliverables at each level of the organization.

As we discussed in Chapter 1, a clearly stated goal is the primary method for communicating to each employee exactly what outcomes they are expected to deliver during a specific period of time. And as we discussed earlier in this chapter, an exceptional manager takes the development level of each employee into account when setting expectations. In essence, every task you assign, along with the associated goal that you establish for every employee in your organization, is a form of delegation. And, if you are going to achieve excellence, the amount of work delegated to each employee must be reasonable and ultimately achievable, based on that employee's job level and capabilities.

So, if there seems to be an uneven or unfair distribution of work in your group, then it might be a good time to revisit the way your organization is designed. Here are a few points that might help you focus on the root problem:

- ➡ If there are not clear task assignments and goals specifying what each member of the team is responsible for, and a shared understanding of how all those individual responsibilities contribute to the overall commitments for the group, you need to fix that problem first.
- ➡ If jobs and responsibilities are well defined but your team is understaffed, your primary problem is not delegation; it's staffing.
- ➡ If your team is fully staffed, but under-skilled, again your problem is not delegation; it's training and/or hiring, and/or job leveling.

Bottom line: if you have a delegation problem in your workgroup, that is, if it seems that work is not allocated correctly, focus your attention on the higher-level issues of organizational design, job design, and goal setting. This approach can enable you to discover and fix an underlying, systemic issue, rather than reacting hastily to a symptom of the problem.

Before we leave this topic, however, I'd like to return to the subject of your own personal workload for a moment.

Aside from everything I've said above, we all know that middle managers have a lot of responsibilities on their plates, sometimes more than they can handle. This is especially true of people who have only recently become managers for the first time or have recently moved up to a new level of management. People tend to be promoted to management roles when they are particularly good at doing the work at a lower level. And because they are confident in their abilities in that previous role, they sometimes bring some of those responsibilities with them. The thinking often goes something like this: "If I've always been the best at doing something, why would I hand it off to someone else, especially if I don't trust anyone else to do it as well as I would?" I have encountered many managers who are struggling to let go of the tactical tasks they are good at and move toward the more strategic responsibilities that they are expected to take on.

If you are struggling with the dilemma of how and when to delegate, a good first step is to consider whether it's because you are reluctant to let go of control, to move out of your personal comfort zone, or because you genuinely aren't confident that a subordinate can be counted upon to achieve the desired result. And, if you do have capable employees but you're still reluctant to let go, is it because the task in question is something you simply like doing yourself, perhaps because you feel you receive positive recognition for how well you do it, and you're unsure what you would be recognized for if you weren't doing it? Again, the solution to that dilemma lies in focusing your attention up a level to consider how your organization is designed and how responsibilities are assigned. At the same time, it is critical to think realistically about the resources you have at your disposal and what they are capable of accomplishing. Which leads us to our next topic…

Avoid Management by Wishful Thinking

In this book, you will see me repeat words like "real" and "actual" many times. This is intentional. In my view, the exceptional middle manager is the one who manages real people trying to solve real problems in the real world, while also focusing on how actual products and services are actually experienced by actual customers.

There is often a considerable gap between the vision of what we thought our organization was going to deliver vs. what we *actually* delivered. Or a gap between what our marketing promotions told our customers they were going to receive, vs. what they *actually* received.

To some degree, this gap is inevitable. In order to compete effectively in this economy, your marketing and sales teams have to make the most compelling, best-case promises they can; it's all about beating the competition. But the place for this type of promotional, idealistic dialog is marketing and sales. The risk comes when it permeates other parts of the organization and impacts how managers perceive their internal operations.

Let me give you an example: suppose the leader of your historically successful organization learns that because your customers are suddenly not happy about something—a product, service, etc.—they're starting to migrate to your competitors.

Your CEO may decide it's time for a new campaign to "get back to our roots," "take the customer back," "make the company great again," or something to that effect. They might charge marketing with launching the vision and messaging around this new campaign, and soon we're all using phrases like "world class," "best in class," "unrivaled customer experience," etc.

Soon, that concept will be marketed internally, perhaps via training sessions, speeches by the execs, posters in the hallways, etc., in hopes that everyone will embrace the new vision and instill it into everything they do. However, all too often the vision is just that—an imagined outcome, a view of how we'd *like* the world to be, not how it actually is. And all too often, the organization isn't actually enabled to achieve that vision. This gap can be the result of insufficient budget and resources, inferior or outdated products or services, inability to compete effectively, too many competing priorities, or simply a culture that has become accustomed to over-promising and under-delivering, hence the term "management by wishful thinking."

The exceptional middle managers, the ones who achieve strategic advantage, are those who recognize the difference between vision and current reality, and fight for what they need in order to deliver on the vision, or push back against embracing a vision they know is not really achievable.

The ineffective manager is the one who "drinks the kool aid," pretends that the marketing vision is achievable (often when they know in their heart that it isn't), and then beats their team up when they can't deliver the impossible.

Another, related outcome of management by wishful thinking occurs among executives who themselves do not fully appreciate the difference between vision and reality. If they haven't come up through the ranks, haven't done the job that you do, and experienced first-hand what it takes to deliver the promised deliverables within whatever constraints there are, then they are vulnerable to a mental process that goes something like this: "I envision it… I want it… Make it so."

This mindset is often revealed in platitudes like "work smarter, not harder," or "you just need to do more with less," or "then the magic happens." Sure, sometimes productivity improvements are possible, and these ideals are achievable. But too often, this kind of language just disguises the fact that the leader sees the need but really doesn't know how to address it, just wants someone else to figure it out, and is not prepared to make the necessary investment of dollars and resources.

There was a very senior exec at my client company a few years ago who, upon seeing a presentation of various alternative options, would often say, "You are a victim of the '*tyranny of the or*'." He meant that you should go and back figure out how to do *everything* on your list, not just this option *or* that one. In response, another wishful-thinking exec promoted the idea that we should all embrace "*the genius of the and.*" These were very high-level examples of management by wishful thinking, and they did not land well with employees who were grounded in the day-to-day realities, which often included budget cuts and insufficient staffing—scenarios where hard, trade-off decisions had to be made every day.

If you will allow me one more story to illustrate this point: that same very senior executive, upon learning that we were not competing well in customer satisfaction polls, decided to put a huge priority on improving the customer and partner experience. In that moment, we all understood that customer satisfaction had become a top priority. We adjusted our behavior and our goals accordingly and our customer satisfaction scores began to improve. However, sometime after that, in a difficult budget discussion, our management team was trying to convince this same top executive that his insistence that we outsource major segments of our customer support programs to offshore locations would reduce our ability to satisfy the customers. In this instance, his response was that cost reduction was more important than customer satisfaction, and that he was willing to lose a few points on the customer satisfaction scale in order to shave operating expense. So, we all adjusted our behavior and our goals again and outsourced major portions of the business, while wondering what the priorities really were. After that, I concluded that I'd much rather meet with this particular exec on those days when he wanted to focus on the customer rather than on the budget.

I usually try to avoid bringing sports analogies into the business world, but I have to acknowledge that I see a similar wishful thinking phenomenon in the sports world when a coach or sports announcer says something like "If we want to make it into the playoffs, we're simply going to have to find a way to score more points." Duh. That "find a way" reference is a perfect example of wishful thinking. You either have a plan or you don't; you either have the resources you need or you don't. Magic doesn't happen very often. Exceptional middle managers know that and insist on having the resources they need to meet their objectives, or they insist on modifying the objectives to align realistically to the resources they have. Exceptional managers do not practice, and they do not tolerate, management by wishful thinking.

Beware of Un-delegation

There is another phenomenon that is closely related to management by wishful thinking that is worth discussing for a moment too. I don't have a clever name for this category but it's all about the practice of un-delegating and taking back control during times of crisis.

In the modern business environment, I think most evolved organizations share a view that delegation is good and that distributing decision-making authority to the lowest appropriate level is a positive thing that we should aspire to do. I certainly agree with this perspective too, but I would submit that for many organizations it is exercised as a "good times" privilege that is too often withdrawn when times get tough.

I have been through many different organizational challenges during my career, ranging from mergers and acquisitions to extreme budget shortages. And here's one thing I've noticed: during good times, execs and managers may do a fairly good job of delegating and trusting their subordinates to make decisions. But during challenging times, it is not uncommon for execs to, in effect, cancel that delegation and pull decision-making and control back to themselves. The "wishful" part of this action is an apparent belief that because this situation is critical, the exec can't trust anybody but themself to make a decision.

At best, this enactment of centralized control might be considered the smartest and fastest way to respond when resources are limited, quick decisions are required, and only someone in a high enough position can have the broad view necessary to see all the available tradeoffs and make the right call.

At worst, this tendency to abruptly centralize control can reflect the fact that management feels threatened, doesn't actually know what to do, and simply wants to prevent anyone from taking any action until they figure out a way to reduce the threat.

Some of the types of decisions that are made during these crisis events are so familiar they may seem reasonable at first glance, but I encourage you to think more critically about the usual approaches and consider whether there's a smarter choice available. For example, it's common during a financial crisis to see, without much warning, an executive mandate such as a hiring freeze, a travel freeze, or some other spending freeze imposed. This freeze might be accompanied by a requirement that if anyone wants to spend money on one of these items—something they were empowered to do only yesterday—they will now have to request permission from a higher level of management, often escalated to a level where the executive has little understanding of the details surrounding the request and little time to give it any attention.

Here's an example: years ago, I was working in a large company that fell on difficult financial times. It was clear that we needed to make some significant cost reductions, including significant layoffs, if we were going to survive. But rather than asking the knowledgeable middle and front-line managers to identify rational opportunities for expense reductions, the top execs in the company, probably assuming that time was of the essence, took it upon themselves to make the decisions. And they literally did it by sitting around a table, looking at org charts for all the different groups in the company, many of which they were not familiar with, and deciding which functions appeared to be valuable and which didn't. The effort was called "activity value analysis." They quickly issued a series of mandates about which departments needed to be eliminated. Following this, as you might guess, managers throughout the organization started pushing back, explaining why this function or that one was actually critical and could not be eliminated. Soon the whole process was in disarray, decisions were reversed, employees were subjected to a lot of confusion, and the needed changes took much longer to identify and implement than if management had delegated the process in the first place, rather than trying to control it.

I can't even count the number of hiring and spending freezes I've experienced, often in companies that actually were not on the brink of financial failure, but had suddenly discovered they were "running hot" from a budget standpoint and needed to reduce spending to get back in line. Admittedly, in some scenarios—finding yourself at risk of bankruptcy for example –harsh, immediate measures like hiring and spending freezes may be warranted. But too often, management is just reacting with a knee-jerk, misplaced mandate because they didn't see the problem coming, don't know why it's happening, and/or don't know what to do other than slam on the brakes. The problem with this type of hasty decision-making is often that no one has done the analysis to determine what the underlying problem really is, nor what impact the ill-conceived, hasty solution is going to have in different work units, nor whether there's a better way to achieve the desired result.

An interesting question to consider is why some organizations always seem to respond to financial challenges specifically with hiring freezes. The obvious answer would be that in many organizations, salary expense is the largest part of the budget and therefore the easiest point of attack if you want to reduce spending quickly. But what if hiring the right people is exactly the solution you need in order to address the challenge you're facing? Or, what if your hiring managers were right in the middle of bringing exactly the right kind of talent into your organization at the moment you recklessly imposed the freeze and unknowingly sent those high-value candidates off to your competitors? Rather than using staffing as a proxy for expense, wouldn't it be smarter for exec management to inform the middle manager of the ROI they need to achieve, and trust them to decide whether the best path is to cut salary expense, delay hiring, or perhaps to pursue a different solution altogether?

Another common budget crisis response occurs when management imposes a standard, across-the-board spending reduction. This is actually a relatively easy decision to make, e.g., "the company needs to cut spending by 20%, so every group in the company must cut their spending by 20%." What could be simpler… or lazier?

During challenging financial times, a difficult but perhaps more enlightened approach could be to determine where you actually should be *investing more* to address your problem, and where you will need to make corresponding cuts in less strategic areas, in order to fund those strategic investments. It could be that some programs need to grow significantly and quickly, while others need to be eliminated altogether. An across-the-board spending reduction may feel decisive in the moment but may actually prevent you from seeing, and from achieving, the best solution for your organization. I have to acknowledge that some tech companies like Microsoft and Apple often do a good job of shifting their investments and their staffing to pursue the most strategic opportunities, while reducing exposure in less strategic areas. Of course, we have to also acknowledge that some companies like these have ample resources at their disposal and can afford to experiment with different strategies.

At the time I'm writing this, inflation is becoming a major global concern, and companies everywhere are exploring ways to control costs and preserve profitability. It is very interesting to observe how different organizations are responding to these challenges. Do they "un-delegate" and adopt a top-down, authoritative approach, or do they involve the workforce in helping to identify the best solutions? There are a couple of very different, high-profile methods—both responding to the same challenges—that are getting a lot of attention in the news feeds right now.

At Meta/Facebook, Mark Zuckeberg and his management team have adopted a hard and threatening tone. According to Reuters, at a recent employee meeting Zuckerberg said he was, "turning up the heat" on performance management to "weed out staffers unable to meet more aggressive goals." He actually said, "Realistically, there are probably a bunch of people at the company who shouldn't be here." Chris Cox, Meta's Chief Product Officer, then added, "The company must "prioritize more ruthlessly" and "operate leaner, meaner, better executing teams."[9] Clearly, Meta has embraced the view that salary expense is the problem and they're going to have to dump staff to maintain profits.

Alphabet/Google, on the other hand, looking at the same economic challenges, adopted a much different approach. According to a recent CNBC report, Google's CEO, Sundar Pichai, reached out to employees and asked them to participate in a "Simplicity Sprint" by submitting their answers to three questions:

→ "What would help you work with greater clarity and efficiency to serve our users and customers?"

➤ "Where should we remove speed bumps to get to better results faster?"

➤ "How do we eliminate waste and stay entrepreneurial and focused as we grow?"[10]

Time will tell which of these companies achieved the best financial outcomes as we come out of this cycle, but at what cost? The world is a complex place. Today we are experiencing post-Covid inflation and supply chain issues, at the same time that companies are struggling to attract and retain staff during the "Great Resignation." It's worth noting that both Facebook and Google have at least tens of billions of dollars in the bank. In other words, neither is on the verge of financial ruin. They can probably weather this financial storm and still be in great financial shape.

Now, imagine what it must be like these days to be a Facebook employee, hearing those ominous threats from management, as compared to a Google employee, being asked to participate in finding solutions for users and customers. And on a subtler note, consider how, in their public announcements, the focus of one of these companies is solely on profits and shareholders, while the other emphasizes employees, users, and customers. What do those messages tell employees, and the world, about the culture of each company?

Just before this book was going to press, another high-profile story hit the daily newsfeed: Elon Musk's acquisition of Twitter. It's too soon to predict how that business venture is going to turn out, but I thought this observation from Robert Reich of The Guardian was very insightful:

> *When Elon Musk bought Twitter for $44bn, he clearly didn't know that the key assets he was buying lay in Twitter's 7,500 workers' heads.*
>
> *On corporate balance sheets, the assets of a corporation are its factories, equipment, patents and brand name. Workers aren't considered assets. They appear as costs. In fact, payrolls are typically two-thirds of a corporation's total costs. Which is why companies often cut payrolls to increase profits.*
>
> *The reason for this is corporations have traditionally been viewed as production systems. Assets are things that corporations own, which turn inputs—labor, raw materials and components—into marketable products. Reduce the costs of these inputs, and—presto—each product generates more profit. Or that's been the traditional view.*
>
> *Yet today, increasingly, corporations aren't just production systems. They're systems for directing the know-how, know-what, know-where and know-why of the people who work within them. A large and growing part of the value of a corporation now lies in the heads of its workers— heads that know how to innovate, know what needs improvement, know where the company's strengths and vulnerabilities are found, and know why the corporation succeeds (or doesn't).*[11]

By focusing too much in the moment on only one problem (profitability) and taking attention off the others (staff retention), a company can risk creating irreparable damage to their organization over the long term.

Most of this section has focused on actions taken by executive management, and admittedly it's often difficult or even impossible for middle managers to influence these crisis-management processes. But if you're better able to understand the level of thinking, analysis, and decision-making that your execs are utilizing, you may be in a position to call out the shortcomings and risks in their plan, and to recommend a more rational approach that will yield better results. As they say, the best defense might be a good offense. For example, when you see the financial challenges occurring around you, and you can predict that financial controls are likely to be implemented soon, you may be able to *be your own agent* and take a pre-emptive approach. In other words, put your own proposal together for how expenses can best be managed in your space, and run that up the line through your management chain before they run something else down the line to you. This opportunistic approach might actually get you a pass when the blanket policies are implemented, and management might even adopt your well-thought-out solution as a best practice for others to follow. That could give you significant strategic advantage. But beware: you don't want to give up too much too soon because there's a risk the blanket policy will apply to you too, and you will end up giving twice. To be sure, prospering during times of financial hardship is a tricky game, but in the best interests of your team, it may be a game worth playing.

Understanding Concept vs. Execution

I've always loved being in on the ground floor when my organization was developing strategies for new programs and solutions. There's so much positive energy in an environment where smart, motivated people have come together to envision how problems can be solved, how challenges can be met, and how opportunities can be pursued. However, working in the world of generating stimulating ideas can often be a much more invigorating experience than being the person responsible for delivering on those ideas.

It's an enlightened leader who recognizes that a group of energized, blue-sky brainstormers can produce a mountain of great ideas way faster than the organization can act upon them.

As yet another example of management by wishful thinking, sometimes we commit ourselves to more than we can handle, and sometimes we keep restating those commitments even when it's clear we will not be able to achieve them. Put another way:

The road to disappointment is often paved with good intentions and bright ideas... that never got acted upon.

A relevant phrase I started using a few years ago was "beware of the management offsite meeting." This was meant to be somewhat humorous but did reflect the fact that it's often at the multi-day, vision-centered, inspirational planning events where we come together and generate flip-charts full of great ideas. And as you've undoubtedly observed, once you're back on the job, many of these good intentions start to fade into oblivion because there never really was the ability to execute them.

When I saw this gap between vision and reality showing up too frequently in one of the groups I managed, I wrote the phrase "Concept vs. Execution" at the top of my office whiteboard. Thereafter, I tried to help our managers understand that ideas are great, but at the end of the day, *execution* is what matters most.

In another group, I handed out small sledgehammers with the word "IMPACT" engraved on the handle, to make the same point.

Bottom line: all the great ideas in the world are worthless if you do not, or cannot, act upon them. As always, we achieve success in the real world via results, and results are the outcome of execution. It's not enough to be on board with a vision or full of good intentions; in the real world, managers manage *execution*. That's how things get done. The manager who understands this simple fact has a strategic advantage over the managers who don't.

Prioritization

One of the most important skills an effective leader can possess is the ability to prioritize, which can be incredibly challenging in any situation where demand exceeds supply. Oddly, we don't see much training on this particular skill.

Several years ago, I was genuinely surprised while attending a management meeting in my company to hear the CEO say, "We are really strong technically and we build great products, but we really suck at prioritization." I thought, "Wow… if the CEO himself admits that, and he's the person ultimately responsible for defining our priorities, shouldn't I be concerned?" It was not long after that I left that company, and not long after that before they went through a painful succession of mergers and downsizings. I can't say that failure to prioritize was the reason for their downfall, but it certainly didn't help.

In my mentoring role, I've often suggested that middle managers take a moment to consider how they prioritize things in their personal lives and then apply the same principles to their business environment. Many of us have had to rethink our personal priorities when demand for our resources exceeds supply. Perhaps you were planning a great vacation when you suddenly realized the roof is leaking and you're going to have to redirect those dollars. Or, your kid got accepted to a more expensive school than you expected. Or a relative has fallen on hard times and needs your help. When these things happen in our personal lives, we reorder our priorities as needed. It may be painful, but it's necessary. The same principle applies in your work environment.

I once worked with a very strong IT leader in the banking world who insisted on an absolute ranking of priorities. His view was that no two projects could share the same priority, and he would refuse to deploy his resources until there was agreement on the project rankings. I can hear him now saying, "There is only one #1." If my department and some other department were both insisting that our project was top priority, he would make us get together and work out the absolute ranking. Somebody had to be #2. It was brutal, but it made sense in the real world. It's important to note that this guy was really good at getting things done as promised, on budget, and on time which, as we all know, is not always the case in the IT space.

By the way, that same guy was also notorious for saying "However long you think your project should take, multiply it times three," and he was usually right about that too.

There is not much more to say about the art of prioritization other than to ask yourself: if I'm not able to absolutely prioritize my deliverables, why not? If the answer is that someone else is unable to make a hard decision or conduct the hard conversation, or we actually don't have enough information to make an intelligent decision, you should go back and try again. This is especially true if you work in a world where an unwieldy, unachievable list of projects have been loosely sorted into categories like high/medium/low priority. In many cases, we can't even address all the items in the high list, so why are we even talking about the rest?

Don't drag your team through the pain of never being sure what's most important, in a world of ever-changing priorities. Keep it simple and keep it real.

Manage Change… Before It Manages You

Because I chose to work in the banking and tech industries during periods of tremendous growth—punctuated by frequent disruptions—I have been on both the giving and receiving side of dramatic change, resulting from numerous mergers, acquisitions, downsizings, strategy shifts, product launches, budget crises, reorganizations, and all the other events that make life in business interesting.

While many job descriptions—and resumes—include a phrase about being comfortable with change, it's often during change that we make some of our worst decisions, on both a corporate and a personal level. It's a simple fact that change in the working world is often viewed and experienced as a potential threat, especially when details and answers are not easy to obtain. And, when people feel threatened, they sometimes become very self-centered and behave differently than when things were stable and predictable.

In times of uncertainty—the threat of organizational change, for example—some people feel compelled to try to gain more control over their personal situation by seizing the reins and changing direction, even when there's no evidence that they are at risk. I've seen several instances where, during a time of budget crisis or organizational change, someone would decide they could no longer stand the tension of waiting to find out how it would impact them, so they "took charge" and jumped to another job, sometimes to another company… only to regret it later.

Similarly, I've seen merger and acquisition scenarios in which the people who orchestrated the deal might stand to gain a lot, but many of the other people in the acquired organization feel betrayed, resentful, and negative toward the acquiring organization for no reason other than that their world has been disrupted. As a result, often what started out as a "perfect synergistic union between two companies with so much in common," turns into a mass exodus and brain drain that no one saw coming. There are reasons that many M&A transactions don't turn out well, and one of them is that the impacted people—the ones who actually build and maintain the assets that make each company so valuable— were not considered carefully enough when the execs entered into negotiations.

Back in the mid '90s, my employer was going through a major, highly disruptive merger. They had the good sense to bring in a professional consulting firm, Pritchett, LP, to help us through the process. I found their support, including a program called "Business as UnUsual," to be invaluable.[12] I came away from that training with a set of principles that have served me well during times of change ever since:

➤ In many change scenarios, the people at the top of the organization are the first to become aware of the impending change, the first to react, the first to settle down and get comfortable with what's coming, and the first to get "on message." As they develop the messaging that will bring successive layers of the organization into the "know," they often fail to recognize that each level of employees are also going to experience those same stages of discovering, reacting, and adapting to the change. It's important to acknowledge that people need to go through that process, rather than expecting everyone to just immediately embrace the vision you've communicated.

→ At the same time, it's a mistake to go too far in holding up the process while trying to give everyone a chance to express themselves, get their questions answered, and get comfortable. Sometimes that is not achievable, and you have to "skate fast over thin ice," as Pritchett stated it. In other words, sometimes the change has to happen, it has to happen now, and we have no choice but to take action. Nonetheless, it's still important to recognize that your employees are going to have to process that information and adapt to the changes.

→ Your best people know they're good. They know they have options and they will exercise them if they don't feel well taken care of. Rather than taking them for granted, assuming that they know you love them and will stand by you through everything, you would be wise to "re-recruit" your best people and enlist their help in guiding the team through the changes.

It is important for managers to recognize that while disruptive changes like mergers and reorganizations can be anticipated and planned, sometimes major change just happens with little warning. At the time that I am writing this, the Covid pandemic appears to be waning, and employees everywhere are rethinking their career choices and resigning in droves to pursue other opportunities (a phenomenon commonly referred to as the "The Great Resignation"). Managers today are suddenly struggling with several concurrent dilemmas: first, how to manage cost in the midst of reduced sales, rising inflation, and supply chain shortages, and second, how to respond to the fact that so many office workers prefer to keep working from home and do not want to return to the office, at the same time that many non-office workers are looking for ways to cross over into new jobs where they can work from home too, or at least work indoors. In short, managers everywhere are struggling to understand how to retain good employees, and hire more good employees, while managing cost and growing the business.

As you are reading this, I suspect that, like just about every business, store, or service provider I encounter today, you may be struggling to fill all of your open positions and praying that you don't lose any more people. And, you may even be thinking about your own career situation and whether it's time for you to take action.

McKinsey & Company recently published a very interest-ing article that addresses the difficulties that hiring managers face in finding qualified employees during what they call "The Great Attrition."[13] Their key finding is that companies tend to keep utilizing traditional hiring methods but instead need to adapt to new realities that will require new approaches. McKinsey surveyed participants in six countries and identified these five different "personas" among people who are either looking for a new job or considering changing jobs: Traditionalists, Do-It-Yourselfers, Caregivers, Idealists, and Relaxers. These groups expressed different needs, expectations, and priorities regarding job-related factors such as compensation, meaningfulness of work, career development, support for health and well-being, and other factors. The insights acquired in this study suggest that hiring managers need to employ new tools and new approaches in order to identify qualified candidates across all these categories, rather than focusing only on the limited group of candidates who respond well to traditional approaches.

By the time you are reading this, the priorities and attributes of the job-candidate universe may have shifted yet again. The key takeaway is that you should ensure that you are using the best available methods to seek out qualified candidates who may not be showing up in your traditional searches. More importantly, you should be working continuously to retain the qualified employees you already have so that you don't have to compete so hard for replacements.

Bottom line: disruptive change—mergers, acquisitions, management changes, pandemics, etc.—causes many individuals to stop and think about their own job security, their probable status in the evolving organization, and their available options. While you're busy thinking about yours, don't forget that everyone on your team is going to go through the same introspective process. They may need more information than you've given them in order to make the best decision they can about whether to stay or to jump ship.

There may have been a time when you could assume that employee loyalty—or inertia—would keep them on board with you. That is no longer the case; today you are going to have to explain the value proposition, i.e., make it worth their while to decide not to leave. That process starts with an honest discussion of the organization's needs, the employee's needs, and agreement that you can achieve a mutually beneficial arrangement where everybody's needs are met.

As you think about how best to "re-recruit" your best employees—and perhaps yourself too—it's important to replace speculation and rumors with facts. This is not the time for an internal marketing campaign or pep rally as much as for a frank discussion of where we are, where we're going, why each employee is important to that journey, and, frankly, "what's in it for them?" In the frenzy of hiring that's going on today, many people are being generously rewarded for changing jobs. You need to articulate in clear terms what the rewards are for your team members staying in the jobs they're in.

If this guidance appears to be suggesting that you spend even more money on compensation and career development programs during difficult times, that's partially true. But if you're truly focused on building a high-performance team, then you may find that a smaller team of dedicated high-performers will serve you better than a larger group of less committed employees who are worried about their current situation and wondering where else they could go instead.

A Model for Managers Who Can't Decide How to Decide

For this section, I will be leveraging a decision-making approach known as the Vroom-Yetton-Jago model that was developed in the 1970s and 1980s and has been modified many times since by many people. Like many others before me, I have adapted the model somewhat to fit the world that I have operated in.

If you've been a middle manager or leader for a while, you are probably already familiar with a scenario in which a decision is clearly needed, and you're the one who has to make it, but you're uncertain whether you should consult anyone else, especially your team members, before you decide.

We've all seen instances in which a leader attempts to introduce change in a work environment and it doesn't land as expected. Sometimes this is because the people impacted by that change could have helped to achieve a better solution but were not effectively involved in the decision-making process.

Conversely, there are times where there is way too much inclusion, discussion, and involvement, especially when the leader actually already knows what they want to do—or must do—and the input received is actually not going to impact the outcome.

The simple fact is that there is no single correct approach for how decisions should be made. Just as with the management style discussion above, the decision-making method used should align to the situation at hand. The following model provides some guidance on decision-making approaches that you can apply in different situations to achieve greater success in business outcomes and a positive team experience.

First, the model identifies five different types of decision processes or "styles," as presented in the following table:

5 DECISION-MAKING STYLES

AUTOCRATIC	
A1	You use the information that you already have to make the decision, without requiring any further input from your team. **You decide alone.**
A2	You consult your team to obtain specific information that you need from one or more of your subordinates. You may or may not choose to describe the problem to them. You solicit information only; you do not ask them for solutions or suggestions. **You make the final decision.**
CONSULTATIVE	
C1	You inform your team of the situation and ask for members' opinions individually, but you don't bring the group together for a discussion. You gather additional information from individuals and seek their advice about possible alternatives and solutions, essentially using them as consultants. **You make the final decision.**
C2	You get your team together for a group discussion about the issue and to seek their suggestions, points of view, opinions, and possible solutions, but **you still make the final decision by yourself.**
COLLABORATIVE	
G2	You work with your team to reach a group consensus. Your role is mostly facilitative, and you help team members to reach a decision that they all agree on. You participate in the discussion as any other member, and you do not use your position as the leader to influence them. **The decision is made by the group, and you not only accept their decision, but you are also responsible for it.**

Now that you understand the five decision-making styles, the following chart will guide you through a succession of questions that can help you to land on the preferred style for the situation you're in. If the diagram looks crazy complicated at first, don't worry; as you step through it you'll discover that it's just a series and yes/no answers that lead you to the recommended style.

8 STEPS TO DETERMINING THE
BEST DECISION-MAKING STYLE FOR EACH SITUATION

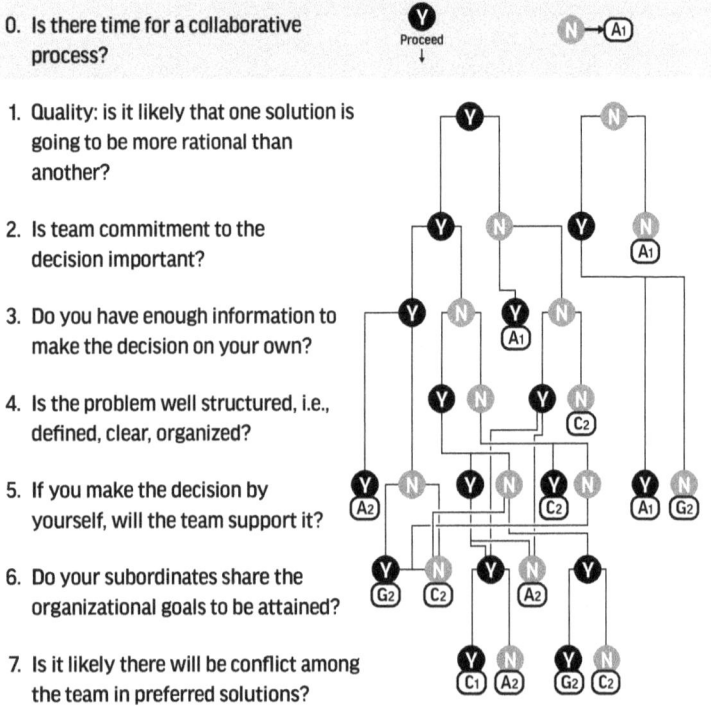

0. Is there time for a collaborative process?

1. Quality: is it likely that one solution is going to be more rational than another?

2. Is team commitment to the decision important?

3. Do you have enough information to make the decision on your own?

4. Is the problem well structured, i.e., defined, clear, organized?

5. If you make the decision by yourself, will the team support it?

6. Do your subordinates share the organizational goals to be attained?

7. Is it likely there will be conflict among the team in preferred solutions?

Note: in the classic model, there are 7 steps. However, I've added step zero to acknowledge that sometimes there is no time to consider a more collaborative approach. Sometimes a leader simply has to make an immediate decision, communicate it, and manage the outcome.

I have discussed the elements of this model with many middle managers who I have mentored over the years, and on occasion it has been an epiphany for them. They discover that there is not just a single right way to interact with their team when making decisions, but instead there's a logical rationale for whether, how, and when you should involve members of your team in the decision-making process. The next time you need to make a decision that will impact your whole team, take this model for a test-drive, and see what you think.

CHAPTER 5
PROJECT MANAGEMENT VS. PROGRAM MANAGEMENT

Most sections of this book are focused on managing day-to-day operations. The purpose of this section is to explore how projects are different from normal operations (programs) and how a different management approach is often needed. So, let's spend some time on the topic of project management.

Whether it's fair or not, a person's reputation in the business world is often based on their success in running a highly visible special project, rather than on how competent they are in running normal daily operations. In fact, it's common to hear an employee complain that someone else benefitted from an unfair advantage because they got to work on a special high-profile project, receiving all that visibility with upper management—while the rest of us slogged away in our day jobs. Unfortunately, there may be a lot of truth to this observation. Sometimes rapid career advancement can be attributed to the visibility attained on one successful, high-profile project. This is why developing project management competency may be very important to the success of your team… and to your own career.

The first requirement for success in project management is simply recognizing that what you're about to work on is indeed a project. Those of us who spend our time in complex organizations, especially in product development, operations, or service roles, are used to working in a world where projects are being conducted all the time. I have often worn the hats of a program manager and project manager at the same time. One thing that came as something of a surprise to me when I entered my consulting career was how many middle managers did not seem to be totally clear about the difference between a program and a project. Sometimes it all seemed to run together in their minds, and sometimes they were trying to apply the same management approach to both areas, often with limited success.

One simple way to think about the difference between projects vs. programs is to differentiate between "build" vs. "run." In an operational setting, the "run" dimension is fairly obvious; it's what we do day in/day out, what's described in the mission statement and job descriptions. The way I'm using the term "program" is with respect to the functional areas and processes you are responsible for, e.g., sales, engineering, security, operations, accounting, etc. Each of these typically encompasses a set of standard processes that are executed in a consistent manner on a daily basis. The confusion comes when it's time to build something new and introduce change into normal day-to-day operations.

This book is not the place to provide an in-depth course in the art and science of project management. Fortunately, there are plenty of resources for that (some companies assign high value to certifications from the Project Management Institute). But I will take a few moments here to offer some hard-learned principles, lessons, and pointers that may be of value.

Somewhere in one of the project management training sessions I attended over the years, somebody made a point that really stuck with me. It went something like this:

A project, by its very nature, is a disruption of normal operations.

For example, we might take a manager out of their normal job to lead an important project. Or, we might put someone in charge who was previously not recognized as a leader on our org chart. The newly appointed project manager must be given the time and resources they will require, often including support from people who work for other managers in the organization. If all of this is not implemented and communicated well, if the project team is not fully supported by management at all times, and the project team members are not totally clear on how they're expected to allocate their time between their project duties and their day jobs, the project can be doomed to failure. Sound familiar?

When a change to normal operations is significant in terms of the time and effort needed to achieve it, the task takes on the dimensions of a project. Sometimes the difference between minor improvements and significant change is hard to detect. Aren't we expected to introduce continuous improvements into the way we do things at all times? Those efforts shouldn't all achieve the status of "project"—or should they?

Clearly, we often make on-the-fly changes and improvements in our normal operations, e.g., simple fixes that don't need to take on all the administrative burdens of a managed project. For example, often the upgrading of office equipment or software, or minor changes in processes or schedules, can be implemented in real time with little effort.

However, in most organizations I've worked in, there was a recurring dilemma concerning when an undertaking should qualify as a project. Typically, we would attempt to set thresholds based on factors like duration of work, number of people involved, budget, or perhaps how many different organizations would be involved or impacted.

I am not able to provide you with a universal rule here; the definition of minor correction vs. small project vs. big project will vary greatly depending on the scale and function of your organization. But if you're going to effectively manage projects and programs at the same time, the question of when it's appropriate to apply a solid project management approach is definitely a topic you should strive to answer in your world.

With that in mind, let's talk about projects and project management and how to recognize when you're in the project space. In large organizations with large-scale project management resources, you might find a team of skilled, professional project managers called the PMO (Project Management Office) or something similar. But in smaller organizations people in regular jobs often have to take on projects with insufficient training and skills, sometimes to the degree that they don't even recognize that the work that needs to be done is actually a project and needs to be managed like one.

Here is a simple illustration I used in my consulting practice a few years ago as part of a concept I called "PMO Lite":

ATTRIBUTES OF A PROJECT

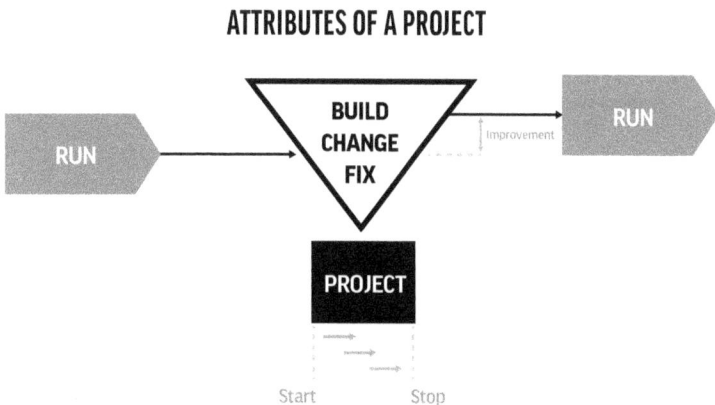

RUN → BUILD CHANGE FIX ⋯Improvement⋯→ RUN

PROJECT

Start   Stop

- Specific objectives and deliverables
- Definite start and stop times
- You can tell when it's completed, and whether it succeeded.

Again, this book is not the place to get into all the finer details of planning, scheduling, and managing projects. There is plenty of quality training and education out there, and plenty of software tools that can improve your capabilities in this regard.

But I can share this one critical finding with you: after participating in countless projects over many years in different industries, surrounded by people with varying levels of project management expertise, some employing sophisticated models and/or software tools—including support from some of the top consulting companies in the world—I arrived at what for me was a profound conclusion:

There are two attributes of a project that matter more than anything else to the success of the project:

Deliverables
Dependencies

Simply put, if you're a project manager who doesn't fully understand what it is you're supposed to be delivering, and if you don't fully understand what other factors—people, resources, technology, data, money—you are dependent upon in order to produce those deliverables, you are likely to fail.

This may be another case where the principle seems ridiculously obvious at first, but I've seen many projects fail because people took off doing a bunch of work before there was clear agreement on what problem they were trying to solve, and what was needed to solve it.

Similarly, many projects fail when they encounter a problem, a barrier—in other words a dependency—that they didn't see coming. Or, they may have recognized that a dependency existed, but they hadn't done their due diligence in the planning phase to verify that the needed resources would be available when the time came. How many times have you seen a project held up because the necessary resources— people, hardware, software, programming support, materials, money, etc.—were not available as anticipated?

The key to ensuring that all deliverables and dependencies are anticipated and accounted for is careful and thorough planning... which is probably the most often-neglected area of project management. Often, under the pressure that managers deal with, juggling programs and projects at the same time, it's common to race through or jump past the planning phase in the belief that we just need to get something done. In fact, I've seen some managers try to put a positive spin on that expedited approach, embracing a "bias for action" or professing to avoid "analysis paralysis." But that's often a coverup for not being willing or able to take time to embrace complexity and think before you leap.

I've seen the "Ready… Fire… Aim" approach cause many projects to fail. I think of the problem this way: if you just parachute into the middle of a project and start taking action without adequate planning, you run the risk that all those things you overlooked are going to catch up with you and you're going to have to stop the project and go back and address them before you can proceed. As one of my coworkers observed long ago, "If we don't have time to do it right the first time, we certainly don't have time to go back and start over."

Bottom line: adequate planning is absolutely critical to a successful project. Don't leave home without it.

One final thought before we leave the topic of project management: if you want to be successful as a project manager, you have to be aggressive in managing "scope-creep." This essentially means that you cannot let people add deliverables or expand boundaries beyond what was agreed to in the original project plan. We've probably all seen large projects, big systems upgrades, or construction projects, for example, that seemed to just keep expanding in scope and never ending, while original promised deadlines and budgets fell by the wayside.

That hard-nosed IT exec I mentioned earlier had a simple method for managing scope creep: once we have agreed on the original plan for a project, then any request to change scope was considered a request for a different project. "If that's what you want, we'll cancel the original project, you can submit your requirements for the new, expanded project, and we'll go back through the process of planning and prioritization." That may seem like a brutal approach, but it did create a culture in which people were very careful and thorough during the project planning phase.

CHAPTER 6
BEFORE YOU TRUST A THIRD PARTY WITH YOUR BUSINESS...

There are a variety of reasons that a middle manager might decide—or be directed—to engage professional resources outside of their company. Perhaps you need to outsource part of your work, to temporarily increase your workforce, or to hire a consultant to assist you with something that is currently beyond your capabilities. There are many ways that this decision to entrust part of your business to a third party can go badly. Let's review some of those risks.

Since the time of my first legitimate business role, working for a large insurance company in Los Angeles, I have had a lot of experience working with vendors. In those days, when everything was still paper-based, I was involved in purchasing mass quantities of printed forms and materials for my company, and I interacted with many large printing companies around Southern California. Later in my career I dealt with another array of printing vendors in the Seattle area, followed by other roles where my teams were supported by call center vendors, fulfillment vendors, software integrators, business intelligence experts, and market research specialists, among others.

I've also had extensive experience working with management consultants, across the spectrum from the major companies like Accenture, Deloitte, KPMG, McKinsey, etc. down to numerous smaller consulting companies and staff augmentation companies.

These third-party companies provide a wide array of different products and services, but the one thing they have in common is that they make their money by doing things that their customers would rather not, or cannot, do themselves.

Outsourcing

Any time you hire a vendor to provide a product or service for your organization, it is most likely for one of two reasons: either it's something you don't want to or can't do for yourself, or you believe that you will get a better cost/benefit outcome by outsourcing. It's worth noting that the same is true of the decisions that many of us make in our home lives, e.g., when to hire someone vs. when to do it ourselves. It could be as simple a task as mowing a lawn or cleaning a bathroom, or as complex as installing a new furnace or replacing the roof.

I have friends who do all of those things themselves, and I have friends who do none of those things—they outsource instead.

Many managers have learned the hard way that when you entrust a portion of your business to someone else, it is easy to spend more time and money than you expected, and to receive less than you expected. But with careful management of your third-party product and service suppliers, you can often greatly improve your business outcomes. Here are some potential pitfalls to be aware of:

In a business environment we often struggle to find the dividing line between "core competencies" i.e., those tasks we think we are really good at and should do ourselves, vs. all that other stuff that we should not, or would rather not do. Typically, the decision to outsource a task is based on the belief that we are optimizing our effectiveness by focusing our internal resources on our core competencies. Yet often this is a rationalization based on fuzzy logic.

First, the term "core competency" has no specific meaning except in the most narrowly-focused type of operation—a tire shop, for example, where the core competencies are selling and changing tires. In the case of larger, more complex businesses, most will actually retain control over some functions that are not their core competency at all, based on the belief that the risk of outsourcing those functions would be too great. An example might be a tech company where the core competencies are writing code and selling software, but where they still have internal departments dedicated to accounting, legal, HR, facilities management, marketing, advertising, etc.

That same company might decide to outsource food services, building maintenance, and even customer service, because those are not viewed as high risk.

In my view, the decision to outsource, regardless of the stated rationale, is too often made in pursuit of lower costs and higher profits, often at the expense of product and service quality, and often at the expense of the customer.

To be sure, there are great vendors out there with great skills, and there are times when it makes total sense to engage them to produce outcomes for you that you cannot produce yourself. But it's also true that every vendor you deal with is a different company with a different set of goals than yours, and too often their primary goal is to separate you from as much of your money as possible.

In truth, vendor management is a skill, almost an art, that many middle managers, even those who deal with vendors every day, have not mastered. If you are in that category, you are at risk of being taken advantage of. So, let's discuss a few of the finer points of good vendor management. Along the way I will occasionally differentiate between general suppliers, outsource providers, contractors, and consultants.

A supplier could be any vendor that you buy something from, either products or services. It's critically important to remember that their company, presumably just like your company, is motivated to make as much money as they can at all times. If you work in a large organization that represents a lot of sales potential for them, they can be very skilled in persuading you that you need to partner with them to ensure your own success.

I've sometimes found it interesting that smart managers who would be wary and cautious in their personal lives—for example when purchasing a new car or hiring a home remodeling contractor—can sometimes be easily duped into falling for a sales pitch from a supplier and entering into a high-cost commitment that is not in their best interest.

As I mentioned earlier, I did a lot of purchasing from vendors in the early stages of my career in the insurance and banking industries. Both are well-established industries with a solid focus on maximizing profits while avoiding risk. The vendors we engaged with in those situations knew they had to meet a demanding set of requirements in order to do business with those companies.

When I crossed over into the tech industry, I was genuinely surprised to see the degree to which many vendors were taking advantage of my company, and how few qualified vendor-management specialists we had on board to prevent them from doing so. After assessing the situation, I concluded that we were especially vulnerable because we had many junior and relatively naïve employees assigned as "account managers" for some large, well established vendor companies who viewed our young and rapidly growing company as a potential windfall.

These vendors were very skilled at influencing our inexperienced account managers via trips, gifts, special meetings, dinners with their top execs, and generally making them feel like very important people—significantly more important in the vendor's world than how they were viewed by our own company. Over time, some account managers started feeling like they were in charge of the outsourced business. They thought of it as their own call center, manufacturing site, etc., sometimes spending more time in that location than ours. We referred to this condition as "going native," meaning the account manager had become more aligned with the vendor company than with ours. Too often, this resulted in our account manager in effect becoming a representative of, a champion of, and an apologist for, the vendor. And this was happening at a time when too many of those vendors were failing to meet our expectations

In order to try to break through that tendency and help our account managers better understand the challenge of effective supplier management, I developed the initial version of the following "Vendor Credibility" chart:

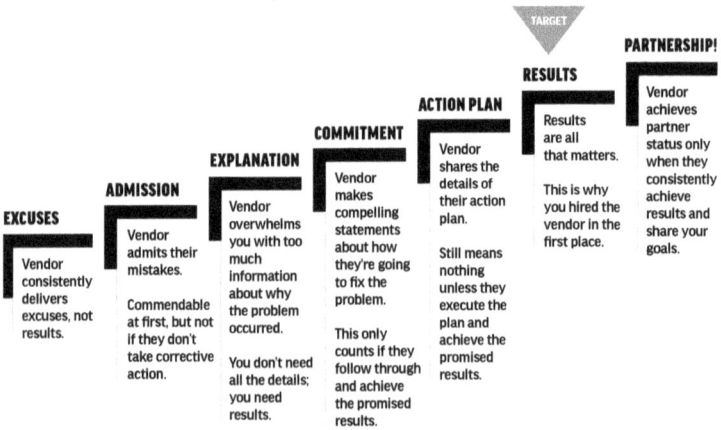

TARGET

PARTNERSHIP!

RESULTS

ACTION PLAN

COMMITMENT

EXPLANATION

ADMISSION

EXCUSES

EXCUSES
Vendor consistently delivers excuses, not results.

ADMISSION
Vendor admits their mistakes.

Commendable at first, but not if they don't take corrective action.

EXPLANATION
Vendor overwhelms you with too much information about why the problem occurred.

You don't need all the details; you need results.

COMMITMENT
Vendor makes compelling statements about how they're going to fix the problem.

This only counts if they follow through and achieve the promised results.

ACTION PLAN
Vendor shares the details of their action plan.

Still means nothing unless they execute the plan and achieve the promised results.

RESULTS
Results are all that matters.

This is why you hired the vendor in the first place.

PARTNERSHIP!
Vendor achieves partner status only when they consistently achieve results and share your goals.

The purpose of this chart was to emphasize that with respect to how we value our suppliers, *results* are the only thing that matters. We hire vendors because we believe they are experts in what they agreed to do for us, and there's really no reason to expect—or accept—anything less than what they promised.

There are a variety of reasons why vendors come up short, and some of them are valid, for example an unavoidable supply chain problem due to severe weather, pandemic challenges, etc. However, I've seen too many situations where the vendor consistently over-promised and under-delivered, where this approach was standard procedure, part of their culture. The goal of good vendor management is to turn this kind of situation around and ensure that your organization is getting no less than what was agreed to and what you're paying for.

Very early in my career, when I myself was one of those young, green vendor managers, I was naively impressed by a particular vendor rep who would readily step up when something went wrong and take responsibility with a statement such as: "You are absolutely right, we really missed the target on that order, and I take full responsibility." Initially I thought this was a stand-up, dependable guy. It took some time for me to realize that his company came up short time after time, and while he was always willing to accept blame for the problem, he never corrected the problem. That's what the "Admission" level of the chart reflects: just admitting responsibility is not the same as delivering the results you promised to deliver. That was an early lesson that helped me to become more adept at getting behind the sales rhetoric and the flattering treatment and stay focused on whether the vendor was delivering on the commitments they had made.

Each level to the left of "Results" is meant to describe some typical ways under-performing vendors respond when they have failed. And while their explanations, renewed commitments, and impressive action plans might seem reassuring in the moment, you should remain laser-focused on the fact that it's *results* that determine your own success. In most instances, you don't actually need to have all that insight into the internal workings of the vendor, as much as you need them to simply deliver what they committed to.

As you move up through the steps of the chart, each level represents a more effective response by the vendor. While some may even seem to be examples of positive behavior, it's important to never forget that anything less than the results you were expecting is a failure on the part of the vendor—period.

Sometimes when we engage a vendor, we like to think of them as a "partner" or an extension of our own organization. I've seen managers take this partner concept too far, believing that we should treat the vendor's employees as if they were our own. Here's another critical point that you should never forget when working with vendors: their employees work for them, not you; their goals are not the same as your goals, and regardless of the language used, only rarely does a vendor actually achieve the level of being your "partner."

Allow me to provide a painful example to illustrate these points: several years ago my team engaged one of the top management consulting companies to help us with a complex, next-generation type of project. They were very expensive, but we initially felt confident that we would be getting world-class support that justified the expense. Over time, however, we began to realize that, even though they had assigned a lot of people to our project and did a great job of managing the relationship and the dialog with us, we weren't seeing the expected results. So, we requested a meeting to discuss the direction of the project. They suggested that we meet at their office for a change, where we could discuss our concerns with their whole team.

As we entered their building and headed for their conference room, I noticed that on the secretary's desk there was a big glass cylinder, about two feet tall, with our name on it, partially filled with plastic balls to indicate how much money they had made off of us thus far that year. Even worse, there was a line at the top of the cylinder indicating their year-end goal for revenue from our account. It was a real slap in the face, and a vivid reminder that their goal was all about increasing their income, about billing us for as many hours as they could and celebrating as their glass jar filled up. I lost a lot of regard for that vendor that day, partially for how greedy they were, and partially for how stupid they were to have that money gauge right out in the open where anyone could see it. That relationship didn't last much longer.

In a different organization where we spent literally hundreds of millions of dollars on our vendors, we were also too often disappointed in the results we received. We had a standard process of bringing the vendors in for quarterly reviews, at which we frequently expressed our dissatisfaction in no uncertain terms. That's when we would hear a lot of the types of responses you see to the left of "Results" in the chart.

Regardless of the vendors' explanations and reassuring promises to resolve the problems, and regardless of their optimistic action plans, too often it seemed like we were having exactly the same difficult conversation every time we met. That's when one veteran supplier manager on our team explained to the rest of us that for the kind of money these companies were making off of us, they were more than willing to come in here once a quarter, let us beat them up, and then make whatever promises they thought we needed to hear, just to keep the engagement going—and the money flowing—for another quarter. Over-promising and under-delivering was a very profitable business model for them, and they were confident we wouldn't really fire them.

To be a savvy buyer and to achieve strategic advantage, you should always remember—just as when you buy a new car—that the vendor is always selling, and regardless of what they might say to the contrary, or the attention and gifts they are lavishing on you, their goals are not the same as yours. Stay focused on getting the results you paid for, the same results the vendor promised to deliver, and don't allow yourself to be persuaded to settle for anything less.

Special Points Regarding Outsourcing of Customer-Facing Services

Over the past twenty years or so, many if not most major companies seem to have outsourced their customer service and support functions, i.e., the very people who talk to their customers most of the time. The typical reason for this is cost savings, and possibly a belief that the vendor has more expertise and can provide attractive economies of scale in running call centers, service centers, support programs, and fulfillment centers, while providing a higher level of service than we can. Sometimes that is an accurate assessment. There are some great vendors out there providing high-quality services all over the world. However, there are also some real duds who are great at selling but not so good at delivering.

It is critically important to always keep in mind that when your customer contacts your outsource vendor, they believe they are talking to you. Here are some key things to consider when looking for a vendor to represent you to your customers:

➔ Rapid growth is a major priority for many outsource service providers and they accomplish much of it via mergers and acquisitions. You should beware of any company that is growing so fast that they don't really understand all the different operational models they've onboarded. I've seen instances where the only evidence that a particular service delivery location is part of the company I'm talking to is a temporary banner over the front door. Otherwise everything going on inside is still what it was before the merger, including processes and systems that don't interface with any other part of the acquiring company.

→ Outsource service providers are very good at selling. They will often put their best people in front of you to close the deal, but then assign a much lower level of talent to support your account on a day-to-day basis. Or, they may assign their A-Team to you while things are ramping up, and then pull them to go launch another account, while they assign their B- or C-Team to support you on an ongoing basis. If one of the reasons you've selected a vendor is the quality of the people you met with in the initial meetings, make sure those people are going to be assigned to your account for a minimum period of time before you sign anything. One potentially revealing question to ask before you commit is what those A-Team members were working on before this, and how long they were assigned to that project and that client, before being introduced to you.

→ Some outsource service providers experience very high turnover, often more than 100% per year! While that may seem outrageous at first glance, it might be a little more understandable when you consider the monotony of what their employees do for the client all day long and how little they get paid for it. However, you should be concerned about a high agent turnover rate for several reasons:

- Many people who work in service centers can't wait to leave phones, chat, and email behind and move into the higher-level jobs where they don't have to interact with customers—your customers—all day every day. Fortunately, for some of them, the vendor company often needs to pull their best employees off the front lines to perform roles where higher-level knowledge is needed, e.g., to build and deliver training programs, serve as mentors, or work on only the most complex "tier 3" issues. The result is that the people at the bottom of their skill hierarchy are often going to be the most numerous, the least knowledgeable, and the most likely to pick up the phone or the chat conversation the next time your customer calls in. That arrangement might work fine for some clients when the service issues don't require much skill, but will it work for you? Make sure you know going in whether there will be enough skill among the first-level agents to handle the types of support that your customers will need.
- Many vendors support multiple clients— possibly including one or more of your competitors—from the same location, and they often reserve the right to move their agents

around from account to account. Think about the implications of people in that service center who know the details of your business taking that knowledge with them as they move over to support your competitors. If that matters to you, you'll need to negotiate up front to ensure your information and intellectual property are secure.

An outsource solution often looks like a good financial move because the vendor's cost per transaction appears to be so much less than yours. Based on economies of scale, this should be the case, but sometimes you end up paying more than you should while getting less than you expected. Sometimes there are some hidden costs in the arrangement. A key to getting the value you expect lies in how you structure the pricing model. You need to keep in mind that the vendor's goal is to make as much money as possible, which is reasonable. But you need to consider which kind of pricing model will also get you what you need. For example, if you're working with a call center vendor, should you pay them by the call, by the minute, by the number of sales they close, or the number of problems they solve? We won't go into a deep analysis of all those options here, but the key point is that you should be keenly aware of what kind of incentives you are accepting and/or introducing into the pricing model and how that might affect the vendor's behavior. For example, if you pay the vendor based on number of calls or chats or emails answered, then they might be incented to keep each call as short as possible and drive as many calls as possible through their system. And this may very well be what they explicitly direct their employees to do. The agent who you think is providing "world-class" support to your customer, may actually be incented to get your customer off the line ASAP so that they can move on the next customer call and rack up some more income. Here are a few observations that might help you identify the best pricing model:

→ I've seen situations where the cost per call was very favorable, but what wasn't obvious was that the agents were rushing calls, even hanging up when a call looked like it was going to be time-consuming, in order to drive their numbers up. The vendor ends up making more money, but If your customers have to keep calling back to get their problem solved, then the call volume is artificially inflated, your customers are unhappy, and you're paying more for the service than you should—possibly more than if you provided that service yourself.

→ Another important factor you should be aware of is how the vendor's employees are evaluated. If they're rewarded based on volume, when you want them to prioritize quality, then your goals and the vendor's goals are not aligned, and you are at risk of not getting the results you expected.

→ The key to success here is to structure the pricing model such that you pay a fair price for the outcomes you need, while allowing the vendor to make a reasonable profit.

This is another great opportunity to remind you to...

"Inspect what you Expect"

If you're not already vigorously doing this with your outsource vendors, I strongly suggest you take up the habit.

One last caution regarding outsourcing: As I said before, these vendors can be very skilled at sales. They also know that most companies are always looking for more ways to reduce cost. At the outset of your outsource solution you might prefer an arrangement where the vendor will provide the staff, but you will control training and quality monitoring to ensure that you're getting the level of performance you require. In other words, you will "inspect what you expect."

As time goes by, however, if your management is enamored with the cost-savings potential of outsourcing, they may encourage you to outsource more of the functions that you still perform, perhaps including training and quality control, so that you can eliminate the full-time staff who perform those functions today and save even more money. And your management may be aware of these opportunities because your vendor, who you thought worked for you, has also been taking your exec to lunch, golf, etc. and pitching them on how to be a cost savings hero by turning more and more control over to the vendor. I've seen this fox-in-the-henhouse scenario happen multiple times and I've always thought it was crazy. In the worst-case example, the vendor hires the staff, develops the training materials, trains the staff, monitors and evaluates the staff performance, makes money at every step, and sends you a bill. You may have had little involvement in any of it and little insight into the experience your customers are having. And don't forget, your customer thinks they're dealing with you.

Bottom line: if you initially outsourced a portion of your business with the expectation that the results you'd get would be as good or better than what you could achieve with your own in-house staff, but at a lower cost, then in my opinion you should retain control of everything that has to do with verifying the activities performed on your behalf, and the quality of performance that you require. Inspect what you expect.

Allow Me to Consult You Regarding Consulting

The first point I must make here is that I have worked with some extremely talented consultants from both the largest consulting companies and the small boutiques. I have seen some of them deliver very high-quality solutions that my company was not capable of producing on our own. In other words, we got our money's worth and I would hire them again and again.

I've also thoroughly enjoyed my own time as a consultant, and I believe my clients have been well served. Having said that, I'm also aware of some potential pitfalls you might encounter when you set out to engage a third party to come into your business and help you solve a problem. As a middle manager, I have spent many thousands of dollars on consultants. When I reflect on the ROI from a number of those engagements, I'd really like to have some of that money back. I will try to help you avoid making some common mistakes.

The scope of this discussion will include all types of contractors and consultants that you may encounter, because sometimes the only discernible difference between them is their tax category, i.e., whether they work for themselves or somebody else, otherwise referred to as 1099 vs W2.

There's a popular saying that goes like this:

"Definition of a consultant: A person who borrows your watch and tells you what time it is."

There is a bit of wry humor in this statement, but also more truth to it than you might like to think. There are two types of consulting scenarios that come to mind in this context:

➤ A project where the consulting company sends in a team of people to study your business, interview you and your people (borrow your watch), compile their ideas into a proposal, and tell you something you essentially already knew (tell you the time).

If that's what you hired the consultant to do for you, perhaps because you didn't have time to interview your people and evaluate their ideas yourself or thought they might be more forthcoming talking to an objective third party, then hopefully you got what you wanted out of the engagement. On the other hand, there may be instances when allocating your own resources is a much more cost-effective approach than paying high-priced consultants to tell you what you already know.

→ A project where the consultant brings sophisticated analysis techniques and models to bear on your business problems and proposes advanced solutions. A solution is a solution, and you may be getting a great one.

Some consultants will provide you with an estimate of the total cost of a project and they will do whatever work is necessary to deliver. But it's also true that many consultants bill by the hour and are incented by their management to log as many billable hours as possible. Sometimes consultants present proven solutions that have been recycled time and time again but are presented as if they're custom-built for your business. (I know this because on occasion I have found some other client's name mistakenly left in the final report that was presented to me... rookie mistake.) Again, you may get a satisfactory solution, but make sure you're not paying for hours of original work if the proposal was just pulled off the shelf and edited a bit.

These days, it seems like the term "consultant" gets applied to a whole array of different kinds of workers. It's important that you know the difference and pay no more than necessary for the level of support you need.

A key point that I have shared with many fellow consultants is this: a true consultant should consult, that is they should know more than the client does about something and should be able to propose solutions that the client could not have come up with on their own.

If you are hiring someone to come into your business and just do production work, perhaps the same work that your current staff do, or a former staff member used to do, that is not consulting; that is staff augmentation.

In the world of business, there is a long continuum of third-party support services that extend from basic, low-cost temporary staffing on one end, all the way to sophisticated, high-priced management consulting at the other end. There are countless businesses of all sizes arrayed along this continuum, and many of the smaller companies in this space call their employees "consultants" when they actually are not doing much, if any, consulting. I have worked in a corporate environment where there are literally thousands of vendor staff on site, many of whom are called consultants but are actually just doing production work, sometimes for years at a time. Some are essentially high-priced "perma-temps."

So the first recommendation I have for you in this regard is to make sure you know what type of support you need in order to address the problem you're seeking to solve. If you just need some more hands on deck to help get the work done, think twice about paying the high cost of consultants who won't actually do any consulting.

If, on the other hand, you have complex problems to solve, and you need to launch a project with really smart people to help you analyze the problems and develop sophisticated solutions, then you may indeed be in the market for a consultant. Here are some thoughts about how you can get a good return on your consulting investment:

➤ Just as we discussed above in the outsourcing section, consulting companies are also very good at selling, and they will often send some very impressive, A-Team level talent out to conduct initial discussions with you. You should always be totally aware of the level of talent that would be assigned to work your account, as opposed to the people you met on day one. If they're sending you a seasoned veteran with a long record of successful projects, then you should expect to pay. However, many consulting companies don't actually have a stable of that kind of talent just standing by, ready to deploy as soon as you call.

- In fact, in more cases than you might believe, the consulting company, especially the smaller ones, may actually have no one available to work on your project—no "bench" of qualified consultants. In these cases, they may actually locate someone to hire only after meeting with you, determining what kind of skill set fits the assignment, and securing your commitment to the project. One could argue that this approach is reasonable in a world where "billable hours" are their only source of revenue and a group of unassigned consultants would be a drain on profitability. On the other hand, this just-in-time practice makes it very challenging for you to know what kind of talent you're paying for. It all comes down to who the consulting company is willing to hire or reassign in order to close the deal with you.
- Many consulting companies will rave about the exceptionally talented people who work for them, and their unique ability to provide you with highly advanced solutions that will help your organization evolve and prosper. However, over many engagements with consulting companies, I've seen this trend: they tend to hire from two populations: young, recent college grads for whom this might be their first real job, and people between jobs—perhaps because they recently joined the Great Resignation or were recently laid off, or their previous company went out of existence, or they just moved into the area. Whatever the case, you

should be fully aware of the background and skills of each person being assigned to your project and billed to you, and you should be confident that you're getting the talent you require and expect.

To be sure, top consulting companies hire capable people, provide lots of internal training and development, and incur the expense of keeping talented consultants on the bench and ready to deploy. Bottom feeders, on the other hand, might make all the same promises but send you someone they didn't even know a week ago.

Therefore, before you sign the contract, ask yourself and the vendor, "Who will actually be working on my project, and how much do they truly know?" Whether the vendor can answer that question on the spot or can't tell you until the contract is signed, you need to retain as much control as possible over the level of talent that is assigned to you. This means you should be able to screen their proposed candidates to verify their qualifications, and to reject anyone who doesn't meet your expectations. And, you should have the same ability if or when the vendor needs to replace one consultant with another. This is not easily achieved, and you may need to build these requirements into the initial contract.

- Consulting companies typically bill you by the hour, and the hourly rate varies by the skill level and seniority of the consultant assigned to your project.

In the more advanced companies, this rate can run to several hundred dollars, or even over $1,000 per hour. And don't forget: the meter is often running at all times that someone in that company is interacting with you or your project—whenever you call or email to ask a question, whenever someone from the consulting company drops by to check in on the project, etc.

Be aware of what you are paying for. Ask about what qualifies as "billable," and then ask for a detailed accounting of every hour billed and make sure it reflects what you thought you signed up for. If you're being charged senior-level rates for someone who purports to be managing the team assigned to you, but you never see any evidence of that person being involved, ask for an explanation, including how many other projects that senior person is "managing" for other clients.

➡ Sometimes consultants and contractors can look like magicians, getting so much valuable work done in a fraction of the time that it would have taken you or your team. But consider this: they have nothing else to do all day except work on your project, while you probably have meetings to attend, people to lead, budgets to manage, etc. etc. Imagine how much you could accomplish if you could focus on one project 100% of the time! But that's not why you got into management, is it? Before you overvalue the support you're getting, it's worth considering whether the results truly are amazing, or are simply reasonable given that a qualified person was able to focus their undivided time and attention on the project. And if you really are getting amazing results, hang on to that consultant!

Here are some additional points specific to the hiring of temporary staff:

➜ When it comes to hiring what is essentially a contractor to augment your team or handle a special project under your direction, there are a few more things you should be aware of:

  ▫ Generally speaking, a full-time employee working for you will be more committed and dependable than a contractor. Beware of the urge to hire a contractor simply because it's the fastest or cheapest way to fill a role or because you'd like to avoid the administrative burden of managing an employee. If you need a full-time employee, do the right thing and hire one.

  ▫ Whenever I hire a contractor—especially a 1099, self-employed contractor—I always ask why they chose this career path rather than a full-time job. The typical answer you'll hear will include something about enjoying a variety of work experiences, along with flexibility to set their own schedules or take time off in the summer. On the surface that sounds plausible, even interesting. However, I have found that this story often doesn't really hold up; most of the contractors I have known actually work full time, throughout the year, and some have been on board with the same client in the same role for a long time.

And here's an even more interesting point: whenever I asked the contractors whether they are actually hoping for a full-time job in our company, they would answer "yes" about 90% of the time! In that instance, the obvious question is why they aren't already working full-time for your company.

Contracting is a legitimate, time-honored method for getting a foot in the door and landing a good job. But it's also sometimes the career path chosen by someone who has had a hard time getting—or keeping—a job. You should know the motivation of the person you are paying to support your organization.

□ Because of the high likelihood that a contractor is actually looking for a full-time position, there is always some risk that they are going to leave you sooner than expected, often because someone else in your company—perhaps even someone who your contractor has been working with on your behalf—and impressing on a daily basis—has hired them out from under you.

The moral of this story is: if what you actually need is a full-time dedicated employee, then hire one. If you actually need only a short-term contractor, then hire one. But if you find yourself in the position where you have a full time, long-term contractor on your staff, you have probably made a mistake. And if you're following that approach because your management thinks they are controlling expense by holding your allocation of full-time positions down while allowing you to spend "vendor dollars" on contractors who are going to be around forever anyway, then you may be trapped in a bad case of "management by wishful thinking," which we discussed in Chapter 4.

➤ One final caution before we leave the topic of third-party support services. Sometimes when you see the credentials for members of the team or individual contractors who will be assigned to your account, you might be impressed by the wealth of experience they bring to the table. And sometimes you will benefit greatly from their experience. I like to think that my clients have.

However, there are instances where someone shows a desirable skill in their resume, but it has been so long since they had exercised that skill that they actually are no longer qualified in that regard. This is an obvious risk with regard to technical skills—coding skills for example. But another scenario to watch for is the contractor who once excelled at the task, but then moved up through management roles in their career, and now, for whatever reason—scaling back, layoffs, etc.—they are presenting themselves as a hands-on practitioner of something they haven't actually done in a long time. More than once, I've seen regrets when someone who fits this profile has failed to deliver, for example when the client thought it was clear the contractor was being brought in as a worker, an individual contributor, but the contractor was looking around for the team they thought they were here to manage. It harks back to that point we made earlier: execs need to be execs.

That's probably enough discussion about third-party service providers. Let's get back to talking about the people who work for you and how to mold them into a high-performance team.

CHAPTER 7
PERFORMANCE ASSESSMENT

Assessment models

Just as with every coach in the wide world of sports, every manager dreams of having a team populated with nothing but high performers. Whether you've achieved that outcome or are still striving for it, you have a critical responsibility to help your team members to further develop their skills and advance in their careers, while they increase their contribution to the success of your organization. You can achieve that kind of positive development only via processes that accurately assess current levels of performance and provide meaningful guidance on how to improve.

Before we talk about the act of executing a performance review, I'd like to spend some time reviewing the types of performance assessment programs that exist across different organizations and encourage you to critically assess your organization's program to ensure you understand how it really works.

Performance assessment is an essential—and often the most difficult—responsibility of any people manager. I've worked within many different performance measurement schemes—many of them developed only after conscientious and painstaking effort by the HR department—and, in my opinion, most of them have been seriously flawed.

It comes down to this: for an employee to understand where they stand, there have to be performance ratings, i.e., universally understood definitions of achievement. But, in order to be effective, those ratings have to be fairly applied, based on actual performance relative to expectations, and meaningful in the real world. This is where many programs—for a variety of reasons—fall down.

The underlying concepts of performance assessment are deceptively simple: the employee was expected to accomplish something; they either did or they didn't, and it's your job to tell them so. Typically, we have a range of ratings we can assign to describe the employee's performance, and they are also simple, at least at first glance. For example, "Meets" should mean a person really meets expectations; "Exceeds" should mean a person truly exceeds expectations, and "Does Not Meet" should mean a person failed to meet expectations.

Obvious, right? A rating system like this may be simple in concept. Yet it can be very hard to administer in the real world of real people, especially if your executives are worried that the company is spending too much on salaries and benefits, or believe their middle managers are being too generous with ratings and compensation while avoiding making the tough decisions.

And to be fair, in the real world, where staff members often believe they're doing a better job—or deserve more rewards—than their boss appears to recognize, managers too often do avoid making the tough decision and having the tough conversation. (We'll talk about the review conversation more in the next section) Bottom line: even in the best conceived and fairest programs, performance assessment is a challenge.

At its worst, there's nothing more painful for managers and staff alike than a performance management system that isn't fair, i.e., a system where managers are not able to be honest and fair with their team members… especially when everyone knows that's how the system works. I know that sounds harsh, but many of us have worked in systems like this.

Often the model design starts off right, with the simple and reasonable notion that each member of the team should be evaluated based on progress made toward achieving their agreed-upon objectives. Nothing wrong with that idea; the "management by objectives" model has been in place in one form or another for decades.

The problem starts when some brilliant person up in the exec level decides that people should be graded on a curve, or "stack ranked," based on a belief that people will be more productive if they're pitted against each other in a head-to-head competition where winners and losers must be identified.

On the surface, the ranking approach may sound smart and aggressive, like a sports team that wants only top talent competing for every position, in order to increase their chances of winning. *(Note: beware of sports analogies in the business world; they can lead to overly-simplistic thinking.)*

However, this kind of forced ranking system can really go off the rails when it's implemented with blunt force such that the ranking process ignores the employee's *actual* performance, focusing instead only on their *relative* position in the stack.

The worst scenarios occur when exec management assumes middle managers can't be trusted to be tough enough, so they impose a fixed allocation. In other words, they dictate that a specified percentage of the team must be allocated to each level, e.g., X% in "exceeds," X% in "meets," X% in "does not meet," or some equivalent brackets. At this point, there are often two conflicting performance assessment schemes trying to co-exist: one that rates a person on whether they actually met or exceeded their objectives, and another that force-ranks the team members into the same categories, sometimes regardless of whether they met objectives.

The obvious problem this approach overlooks is simply this: any manager worth their salt will try their best to populate their team with the very best talent they can find. However, if you're lucky enough to build a team of top performers, when the time comes to stack rank them, if you have to meet quotas for each performance level, then you may have no choice but push satisfactory performers into lower levels than they earned. And now you've got a major problem to manage.

Seriously, I've seen too many situations where a manager had to conduct a performance review discussion that went something like this:

> *"Billy Bob, I want you to know that you've done a good job, you've met your objectives for the year, and I really appreciate your contribution to the team. However, as you know, we have to fit everyone into the stack rank and after comparing you to your teammates, I have no choice to put you in the "does not meet" category. Consequently, you won't be getting a salary increase or a bonus, and you really need to get your rating up before your next review (presumably at somebody else's expense), or I may have no choice but to remove you from the team..."*

You think that sounds crazy? Hey, it gets worse. I worked in one company where a Senior VP embraced this stack ranking mentality in a big way and mandated that every team had to be stack-ranked, and at the end of the review period, the bottom fourth of the stack should be terminated—period—and then replaced with new people performing at the top of the next stack rank. He did not allow for the fact that on some teams everyone could be meeting or exceeding objectives. Instead he espoused a blind and theoretical belief that if you follow this practice—no matter who gets hurt or demoralized by it—the company will benefit from an ever-increasing level of talent. Of course, it didn't work, and we managers tried our best to finesse our way around it. But it did succeed in creating a lot of unnecessary pain, turnover, and morale issues in the company.

This is yet another example of management by wishful thinking. As you and I both know, those superstar players that every manager longs to hire for every position simply aren't available, or don't even exist for every role. In the real world, virtually every manager is continuously in the process of developing their team members, and there's always someone on the team—sometimes every member of the team—not yet performing at the level you're hoping they will achieve in the future.

In the midst of all this negative perspective on performance management programs that I have experienced in the banking and tech industries, I have to mention that I also worked for one company where the performance assessment system was especially enlightened and fair. That company employed the typical Meets/Exceeds/Does Not Meet grading scale, but it was applied in a way that was honest, fair, rational, and much more effective than a forced stack-rank.

First, managers were both taught and trusted to do the right thing. In addition, there were one-over-one reviews by their managers, and sometimes by HR, to ensure the quality, fairness, and cross-org parity of the reviews.

Secondly, there were no quotas. If you truly had a team of superstars, they were all eligible for the rewards they deserved.

Finally, this HR department understood that things can get out of whack in the ever-changing people sphere.

If a manager believed their team wasn't leveled correctly, or salaries weren't distributed correctly, or someone deserved a promotion at an unusual point in time, they could go to HR, make their case, and changes could be made. In other words, this HR group was committed to doing the right thing, even when the right thing in the moment may have been a little out of line with the general guidelines. It was a refreshing contrast to most other HR programs I had seen before or since, and it set a new standard for me around how to manage the people dimension of an organization. And oh, by the way, this company had the highest employee morale and the most enjoyable internal culture of any company I've worked for.

Even when you have a good performance-management model in place, however, the real challenge is for each manager to implement and execute that model as intended. Sometimes this can all look simple and straightforward on paper. Yet human nature is a powerful thing, and even in a well-designed and fair system, accurately assessing the quality of another person's efforts can be a challenge for many of us. In the next section, we'll focus on the task of delivering and discussing your assessment with each member of your team.

Conducting Performance Reviews

As mentioned above, conducting performance reviews is one of a manager's most difficult tasks and many of us aren't very good at it. For many of us, it doesn't come naturally. It's a skill that must be developed, and the sooner you develop it, the sooner you're going to be comfortable and effective in your management role. I believe there is a short list of guiding principles that can help tremendously in this regard:

- ➤ Tell the truth, and tell it often.
- ➤ Base the assessment on previously and mutually agreed-upon objectives.
- ➤ Make sure those objectives are based on outcomes, not activities.
- ➤ Make sure there are no negative surprises for the person being reviewed.

With respect to getting the outcomes you desire, managing people can sometimes be a lot like parenting. The sooner you tell the truth and drive for the desired behavior, the sooner you're going to get to where you need to be. Conversely, the longer you pretend that things are okay when they're not, the deeper the hole you will dig, and the more likely it is that you will never achieve your desired outcome.

Put another way, the best managers are the ones who care about people but are also effective in delivering criticism. Being honest about a person's performance shortcomings is difficult, but the sooner you get comfortable with it, the sooner you will succeed as a trusted and respected manager, coach, and mentor.

Somewhere along the line, when I was managing managers and reviewing their reviews of their employees, I started to notice a subtle pattern in the performance reviews I was reading. I dubbed it the "soft middle," and it typically looks something like this:

"Sally Sue did a great job on A, B, and C during the review period. Thank you Sally! Going forward, Sally needs to focus on improving in the areas of X, Y, and Z."

The more I saw this recurring pattern in written performance reviews, the more I recognized that something was missing. If Sally was doing so great, then why was there a need for improvement? Was there something going on here that we weren't talking about—something in the middle between good things that happened in the past and improvements that needed to happen in the future? In other words, is there something going on *right now* that the manager isn't satisfied with but is avoiding talking about? Hence, the "soft middle."

We managers are only human. Just as in many social conversations in our personal lives, we often avoid the raw truth, choosing instead to say things in more positive or vague terms than we should. But when we do this, our employee walks away from the review either confused or thinking that they're doing much better than they really are. That's a recipe for a negative outcome down the road.

Many employees who are terminated from a company can look back on a succession of good reviews and lots of positive statements from their managers, sometimes even including promotions and rewards. And now, feeling angry and betrayed, they can only wonder why they didn't see the end coming and who didn't tell them the truth when they needed to hear it?

For the exceptional middle manager, it comes down to being courageous—an important quality of all successful leaders. If you want to foster the development of high performing, confident and motivated employees, you need to tell the truth about the past, tell the truth about the present, and then tell the truth about what you need to see in the future. If there's something going on that you're not happy with, the sooner you address it and resolve it, the sooner the employee can improve and advance to the next level.

You can avoid the "soft middle" in the reviews you write by making sure there's a section that starts with a phrase like "At this time…" or "At the time of this review…" and then goes on to talk about the plusses and minuses you're observing *today*, before going on to talk about what you'd like to see in the future.

That point about avoiding surprises is really important. The employee should know at all times how they're doing. If you have not had that conversation with them for a year, and now you're going to tell them something they didn't see coming, shame on you (unless it's a promotion, of course). Seriously, the exceptional middle manager is one who meets with their employees frequently and provides honest feedback along the way, so that employees can continue to adjust and improve their performance. The annual performance review should simply be an official, documented record of the conversation you've been having all along.

Often, employees come into the discussion focused mostly on their overall rating and whether they will get a desired salary increase and/or a promotion. It's fine to start a review discussion with praise for achievements that met or exceeded expectations. But then it's important to make sure the employee hears what you have to say about areas where they have not met expectations. When you start off the discussion saying "good job!", that may be about all they hear, so if you have concerns you need to discuss, you need to make sure the employee understands you are switching gears now, and they need to listen and to understand what action is needed on their part to get to a higher level of performance. It can be helpful to break down the job into meaningful categories and talk about whether the employee met or exceeded expectations in each category. For example, a sales professional might have exceeded expectations related to their sales quota, while not meeting expectations with regard to customer satisfaction.

It is the often-difficult job of the leader to both praise the achievements, and at the same time provide clear guidance on where improvement is needed to bring the overall rating up. The more you do this fairly and consistently across your workgroup, the more your team members can be comfortable and confident that they understand how the system works, and what they need to do on a personal level to get ahead.

Perhaps the most important point regarding performance assessments, and one that I have stated again and again, is that you must strive to differentiate between *outcomes* and *activities*. This topic is discussed in depth in the goal-setting section (Chapter 1), but it's important to note that if you didn't set clear, achievable goals up front, it's going to be very difficult to deliver an objective, defensible review when the time comes. At the end of the day, it's *results* you are looking for, and the person you're reviewing is presumably accountable for delivering some of those results. Sure, they should do so with the right attitude, good work habits, and good communication skills, but if those are the only things you talk about, you're avoiding a key question: did they or did they not deliver what they agreed to deliver at the outset of the review period? Did they meet, exceed, or not meet the expectations that you both agreed upon? Tell the truth.

The differentiation between activities and outcomes may seem obvious at this point, but here's a scenario that may not be as obvious to some of you: I've seen countless situations where objectives and expectations were well documented at the outset, but when review time came, the written objectives were largely ignored and the review was written in a more subjective, unsubstantiated manner. In other words, the performance management tools the manager needed were right there, but they didn't pick them up and use them. This is often because those original objectives, sometimes written more than a year before the performance review date, were no longer applicable in the current situation. This can happen when there are changes in budgets, targets, project scope, organization structure, etc., and no one goes back to adjust the goals to reflect those changes. The world has changed, and the employee has actually worked on something other than what was anticipated in old objectives that now seem irrelevant.

If this sounds like a familiar scenario to you, make no mistake: it is the manager's fault that performance objectives were not taken seriously and were not updated regularly to reflect reality. When that happens, you can find yourself in a position where you and the employee are trading subjective opinions about whether they met or failed to meet expectations that were never clearly documented and communicated. It pains me to think about how often I have observed this very situation, and how often it is the employee, not the manager, who suffers the consequences.

What to do about That Problem Employee? Conduct a Cost/Benefit Analysis!

Any manager who has been leading teams for even a short a period of time will likely have been faced with the challenge of dealing with a difficult employee. Sometimes the difficulty is based on the fact that expectations have never been clearly communicated and the employee has a different view of their role or status than the manager does. Sometimes the employee and the manager simply don't get along, and they're never going to. Sometimes the employee is a chronic non-performer, and they should be terminated—more on that below.

On the other hand, sometimes the difficult employee is a good performer, perhaps even a top performer, but their presence on the team—their attitude or behavior—is having a negative, disruptive impact on the manager and/or fellow team members. What's a manager to do?

First, it's important to recognize that you're only human. When someone doesn't like you, or is even openly hostile toward you, you are likely to experience some negative emotions, and it may be difficult to act in a rational, responsible, mature manner. In a situation like this, it's useful to employ an objective, fact-based approach that can help you to separate fact from emotion and get to a genuine solution as soon as possible.

Consider this: when a manager is evaluating the purchase of new equipment or supplies for their team, it is totally expected that they will consider whether that purchase is going to pay off, i.e., to ask whether the cost will be worth the benefit. It may seem a little unorthodox, but I suggest that you conduct a similar cost/benefit analysis of the problem employee, and literally consider whether the cost of keeping them on the team exceeds the benefit that they deliver.

Of course, for this approach to succeed, you will have to bring as much objectivity to the matter as you can. Try to set your personal feelings aside as you look for empirical evidence of positive and negative impacts. Look beyond yourself, and perhaps beyond your team, or even your company, in your search for information. Are you the only person experiencing the problem or is it widespread? Are other members of your team, or even external stakeholders or customers being impacted? Would the absence of this employee create a problem or solve a problem?

If you decide the challenging employee is a keeper, then it's time to apply the truth-based methods described above in order to help this employee find the path to exceeding your expectations.

In the case where you suspect that the cost of keeping a problem employee exceeds the benefit, there is only one more question to ask: can they be turned around and converted from a liability to an asset? If you have conducted the types of honest conversations with this employee that we have discussed earlier in this chapter, you should already have a good idea of whether they are ready and willing to make any effort toward improving their ability to meet your expectations. (If you haven't had those difficult conversations, go back and do so now.) If you're convinced that despite a reasonable effort on your part to correct the situation, this employee can simply never be a positive, productive member of your team, then it's time to consider how to move them out of your organization.

And that brings us to another of the most difficult tasks you will face as a manager: terminating an employee. In fact, it is so hard to do that far too many managers will avoid it for as long as they can. This is a huge mistake, one that can cause lasting damage in your organization.

I won't spend time here talking about all the steps you may have to go through in your organization to build a case for effectively terminating an employee, since that will depend in part on your company's specific policies. But here's one piece of advice: make sure your HR department is on board with your approach and validating your actions every step of the way. Another bit of advice: as you go through the process, keep a picture in your head of what it might be like if a disgruntled former employee files a lawsuit against you and your company. You would have to demonstrate to a courtroom that you had a compelling justification for the termination decision and that you followed all the guidance that was specified by HR. If you go by the book, you should have nothing to worry about; if you go with your gut, you could end up in much worse shape than the non-performer you fired.

In Chapter 3 we discussed the importance of filling open positions quickly, hiring the best talent you can, and re-recruiting your best people. Even when you're doing a good job in these areas, there's one thing that can seriously damage team morale: knowing that a co-worker is clearly not doing their job, and observing that the manager isn't doing anything about it. Whether the team thinks you're playing favorites or that you don't have the courage to do the right thing, you risk losing their trust and respect if it appears you're putting avoidance of your own discomfort ahead what's best for the team. And the converse is often true too: when you take appropriate action to remove a bad performer from the group, the rest of the team members can't help but take notice, respect you for caring about fairness, and perhaps even step up their own game a little.

If you do not know the policies, rules, laws and regulations related to terminating an employee in your country and your organization, you need to skill yourself up in this area. It is a key responsibility of a manager to fully understand and execute these processes in a manner that is honest and fair and does not create risk for your organization.

As we leave this uncomfortable topic behind, here's one final guiding principle that every high-quality middle manager should embrace for the duration of their career: don't ever dump your non-performing employee on another group in your company as a way of getting rid of them. That is unethical, and you're undermining the overall success of your company. Instead, do the right thing; that's why they pay you the big bucks.

And, as a counterpoint to that last point, if the employee in question is actually a talented person who can provide real value somewhere else in your organization, then you can do a real service to that employee and to another team by helping them land in the right role. In Chapter 9, I talk about job "fit." Sometimes a person is simply in the wrong job (i.e., the "fit" isn't right on your team), but they have great potential that could be realized elsewhere in your organization where the fit is better. Again, do the right thing.

CHAPTER 8
HOW TO SURVIVE AND PROSPER IN EXEC PRESENTATIONS

This section is devoted to a phenomenon that is particularly well known in large organizations: the dreaded presentation to a senior executive. However, many of the points made below can be applied to any situation where you need to communicate to someone, especially if it's a person in a position of power relative to you, and you feel nervous or at risk in some way.

I will spend considerable time on this topic because I know how important executive communications can be to middle managers and other team leaders in terms of their sense of job security, job satisfaction, and career potential.

In the early days at Microsoft, making presentations to execs was a scary endeavor. Early in his career as a young leader, Bill Gates was known for responding to proposals with "That's the stupidest idea I've ever heard!" In fact, several of the senior execs I've known in that organization have mentioned that very phenomenon and had experienced it themselves. There were legendary stories of epic failures in this regard, and we managers all knew that careers could be made or lost in a single exec presentation.

Early in my own career at Microsoft, I was once part of a team representing a customer support group when we were making a major presentation to Bill Gates and other top execs regarding how our team could help the product groups improve the quality of their products. We thought we had a very compelling story to tell, and Bill did respond well to some of our discussion about where customers were having difficulty with our products. But right as we were about to land our request for greater involvement in the product development decisions, one of the other senior execs looked right at us and said, in effect, "Don't even think about asking to insert yourselves into that process." And that was the end of the discussion. In that instance, we obviously didn't have a clear understanding of our audience and how they viewed our role.

A couple of years later, I was leading another program focused on doing a better job of listening to our customers and responding to their concerns. We needed to make a major proposal to the executive leadership team regarding a better way to respond to customer complaints. This time, we did a much better job of building our case, and enlisting the support of senior management, to the extent that a couple of the execs who supported our proposal ultimately sold it to the rest of the leadership team. In this instance, we had developed a much better understanding of our audience and what it would take to persuade them to support our proposal.

Later, in another role, I was helping to lead a management development program for a very large group at Microsoft. We had dozens of managers who were striving to improve their management and leadership effectiveness, including their ability to communicate effectively to execs. One creative idea we came up with was to actually interview some of those intimidating senior execs and get their honest perspective on what it takes to effectively present to executive level management… in other words, simply ask them how best to persuade them, impress them, and secure their support. We predicted that having senior execs themselves advise us on what does and doesn't work would to be a huge advantage… and it was. I learned a lot from those sessions and since then have had the opportunity to put some best practices into motion and observe their impact. In this chapter, I'd like to share some of those best practices with you. Hopefully, this material will help you to think like an executive and better anticipate their needs.

Think About Your Audience

One strong, recurring impression I've come away with whenever working with senior execs is that they are extremely busy people, often juggling way more issues than they can keep track of. Your business may be part of their domain, but they have a ton of other things to think about too. Before you ask for a piece of their precious time, think about what they have on their plates, what their —not your —priorities are, and how your topic could benefit them.

Things to remember:

- ➼ The exec may not remember who you are, what business you manage, or what information you may have shared with them in the past.

- ➼ The exec may know less about your business than you assume, especially if they are not involved with it on a daily basis.

- ➼ When working with people in all types of situations, I often observe that "each of us is the center of our own universe." When it comes to presentations, we too often want to tell the world what I call "the story of me" or "the history of my program." In an exec presentation, it's important to focus only on what they need to know; keep it brief, succinct, and compelling.

- ➼ Busy execs are human beings too. Some of them, especially in a fast-growing company, may have been in their current position for only a short time, and some may not in fact have much previous management experience. The exec expects you to be an expert on whatever topic you've come to discuss. So, be that expert and act like it. Be ready to educate the exec as appropriate so that they can provide the response you're hoping for.

➤ As the old saying goes, "You only have one chance to make a first impression." Think about the presentation from the exec's perspective and you'll have a much better chance of success.

Be Clear About the Purpose of the Meeting

Many execs spend most of every day moving from meeting to meeting. Again, they may not remember why they are attending your meeting, nor what you are asking from them. You need to remind them of the purpose of the meeting, what it is you hope to achieve, and what their role is in your meeting.

One of the worst things you can do is to create confusion by cobbling together a bunch of disparate information that makes it unclear whether you're there simply to share information or whether you're actually asking for something. This often happens when people repurpose slides from various past presentations rather than create slides that are specific to the exact topic that they're addressing at this time. If you ever noticed that you are hiding or skipping across slides in your presentation because they suddenly don't seem applicable to what you're trying to say, you may be guilty of this practice.

Of course, the first priority is that you yourself know the purpose of the meeting. In large bureaucratic organizations it's not uncommon for employees to see any opportunity to get in front of an executive primarily as a career-enhancing opportunity, a sort of "audition." Unless it's just a getting-acquainted meeting, that is the wrong perspective to go in with.

The execs are not your casting directors; they are busy managers with many problems to solve. Your objective should be to assist them in solving a problem, sometimes by making them aware of the problem, sometimes by proposing a solution, sometimes by making them aware of an opportunity that they shouldn't pass up, lest it become a problem.

Bottom line: If you want to make a good impression and thereby enhance your career prospects, do so by making it very clear why you're requesting this meeting and then demonstrating how you can help solve problems and capitalize on opportunities. And, from the outset of the discussion —or, better yet in the meeting invitation —make it very clear what role you are asking the exec to play, i.e., just listen and learn, share their ideas with you, make a decision, provide resources, or something else.

Don't Start the Discussion Unless You Know Where You Want to Go and How You Want It to End

When you put several execs in a conference room and start sharing information with them, they are naturally going to start asking questions… it's what they do. It's not uncommon for their questions to redirect the discussion into topics that are outside of the intended scope of your presentation. When that happens, you will get much more respect for keeping the meeting on track than for attempting to chase all the unrelated questions until time has run out and nothing has been accomplished.

One of my own long-standing guidelines for important meetings is that you should always know, going in, what success would look like when the meeting is done. Sometimes it's all about securing approval, money, or staff. Sometimes it's about effectively delivering information. I've been in many situations where my team was determined to get to a certain slide in our deck before time ran out. When we were properly prepared, everyone on my team in that meeting understood and supported the objective. We all helped to avoid time-consuming tangents or moving irrelevant topics to the "parking lot" to ensure we got to what we called the "money slide" and had sufficient time to fully explain what we needed.

When we left those meetings, it was very clear whether we had delivered our message and met our objective, or had gotten blocked or redirected in some way.

Who's the Decision Maker?

If you're setting up a meeting in an attempt to secure a decision, it's very important to know who the appropriate decision maker is for any problem you're trying to address. Sometimes we middle managers simplistically think that if we can just cut through the bureaucracy and bring our issue to the attention of a top exec, we can get the decision we want without having to go through all the intervening levels of management. This can be a serious error.

Paradoxically, while we middle management players might view the top exec as the all-knowing, ultimate decision maker, top execs often don't see themselves that way at all. Execs often believe that there's someone else in their organization who should be responsible for most routine decisions, and that it's only rarely that a decision should be brought to their level. If you have ignored the chain of command or have unknowingly jumped across decision-maker levels in bringing your issue to the attention of the top exec, you may actually be creating some genuine discomfort at that level and not doing yourself —or your career —any favors.

In reality, there should be relatively few decisions that have to go all the way to the top exec. If that's not true in your organization, you may be in a situation where delegation of decision-making isn't clear, or the exec simply doesn't trust anyone else to make decisions. Whatever the case, it's important for you to understand how decisions get made in your organization. If you don't know, you should educate yourself on this topic.

And, if you actually don't know who the decision maker should be for the issue you want to address, don't set up the meeting until you figure it out and can make sure your presentation is directed at that person.

The key takeaway here is that along with clarifying the *purpose* of the meeting, you should not forget to identify *who* should be attending the meeting and then make sure they are prepared to respond to the topics you will be discussing.

Be Succinct; Avoid "Death by PowerPoint"

I recognize that some of you work in organizations where slide presentations are not the norm, or in the case of Amazon, are not even allowed. But for many of us, and especially at Microsoft where PowerPoint was invented, communicating to management is almost always accomplished via a slide presentation. Whether, in your world, the message is delivered via slides, a text-based document, verbally, or whatever, these guidelines still apply.

Across the companies I've worked for, I've seen presentations that have literally contained dozens of slides, even more than 100. And, when people were asked to scale it back, I've seen innumerable examples of what we came to call "quadrant" slides, which essentially meant dividing a slide into four sections and squeezing what was previously a single slide into each of the four quadrants… a 75% reduction in the number of slides! Of course, each slide was like an eye chart at that point, so some execs actually had their assistants print the slides on 11x17 paper so they could read them! This isn't just a rookie mistake; I've seen some VP-level execs following this practice, influencing many of their middle management disciples to adopt this approach and employ it for years. And yet, when I've talked to more senior, highly successful execs, not one of them have supported this approach. Instead, they consistently emphasize how important it is to refine your points and be succinct. Here are some specific tips that execs have shared with me over the years:

➥ The worst thing you can do is have a massive slide deck The exec doesn't have time to richly understand the detail, and can't help you.

➥ Don't make your slides really dense; that suggests you are overly focused on tactical details and don't have command of the strategic aspects of your business.

➥ More words do not indicate more thought; it indicates less thought. Spend the time to simplify what you're presenting.

Know Your Stuff

Perhaps the most career-limiting moment you can suffer is when an exec asks you a question that you should be able to answer, and you can't. Simply put, you should not have gone in there if you weren't prepared. If you want to achieve exceptional middle manager status, you must never let that happen. Here are some simple guidelines:

➥ When you put information on a slide, your audience assumes that you know all about that topic and are prepared to discuss it. All your homework should have been done before the meeting.

➥ When you come into a meeting asking for an executive decision, you're expected to be an expert in your area. It shouldn't be possible for the exec to ask a question that you haven't thought about.

➥ You should come to the discussion armed with solutions to the problems you're discussing. Or, you should make it clear that you don't know what to do and you're looking for input, after which you'll go back and solve the problem.

When exploring this topic with senior execs, I've seen another common thread: execs don't like it when you bring them a problem, dump it in their lap, and expect them to solve it for you. In short, the exec assumes that you have a full understanding of the problem space you're talking about, and that you already have a point of view regarding the options for solving that problem.

Another approach that can help in your preparation is to conduct what has been called an "objection clinic" or "rude Q&A" session. In other words, spend time before the meeting considering what kinds of questions might come up, especially from someone who's more knowledgeable than you, or who's possibly even hostile to your position and may want to throw you off your game. Once you've identified those questions, prepare yourselves to respond to each one —perhaps even via a role-playing exercise —to ensure that you will be poised and ready to respond when the question arises.

Finally, here's an invaluable bit of advice I once received from a senior exec: sometimes in a meeting the exec may want to do a deep dive into a specific area, perhaps due to their own expertise or interests. Before you just jump in with a response, pause for a moment to consider what's actually being asked, and then answer that question instead of blurting out the first thing that pops into your head. I found this to be very interesting guidance, and wondered how often, in my exuberance and desire to impress, I may have made that mistake myself.

Control Your Meeting, and Don't "Bury the Ask"

Even when you've planned well, communicated a clear purpose for a meeting, prepared your team, and are certain you have everything under control, things can still go off the rails. Perhaps you have already had the experience of being in a meeting where you expected to submit a very important proposal or request to a senior executive or other important person. And then for some reason the meeting came to an end without you ever having gotten to that part of the presentation. This happens when attendees get distracted, go off on tangents, or "rat-hole" on the wrong topic until there is no time left for you to discuss your request. That is especially painful when you know that you're not likely to get another opportunity to meet with that exec any time soon.

I've been in meetings where someone, typically an exec's personal assistant, required us to provide printed copies of our presentation. All too often, before the presenter could even get through their introduction slide, the exec or someone else would start leafing ahead through the printed slides and finding things to ask about that were way out of phase with what the presenter was trying to focus on in the moment.

So, how do you keep the meeting on topic, and on track toward achieving your objectives? Here are a few more recommendations that should help:

→ If there is something you are asking for – money, staff, authority, support, etc. – don't bury the request so far down in your presentation that you might never get to it. Identify that aforementioned "money slide," the one that you absolutely must get to if you're going to achieve the outcome you want at the end of the meeting. And as the meeting progresses, make sure you continue to course-correct as needed, to steer the meeting in the direction you need it to go and get to the money slide and deliver your request.

→ Often the smartest approach is to expose your request at the outset of the presentation, or even to embed it in the meeting invitation. For example, in the meeting invite and/or the introduction to your presentation, you could lead with a statement like, "At this meeting we will be asking you to approve X, and we will provide you with the information that supports this request."

→ Try to avoid distributing printed copies of your slides. This will enable you to control the sequence and pacing of your presentation and take the audience to what you want them to see, when you want them to see it.

→ More than one exec has told me they don't mind getting a summary of your presentation strategy before the meeting, so that they already know what you'll be talking about and what you'd like to accomplish. Then they can come prepared with appropriate questions. This approach may not be standard procedure in your world, but perhaps you could introduce it. That could be a huge strategic advantage for you.

→ While any middle manager might find this prospect challenging, many execs would agree with this guidance: don't be afraid to share bad news. Tell the exec we made a mistake. Tell them why we didn't succeed, what we have learned from it, and how we can do better going forward.

→ When proposing your preferred solution, and when applicable, it's sometimes important to acknowledge that there are other leaders supporting other solutions. You might achieve strategic advantage by inviting those other people into the meeting so that the exec can get a full view of the problem space, and the available solutions, and then make a more informed decision.

→ Execs value people who have the conviction and courage to get their ideas across. Don't be afraid of controversy, and don't hide who you are. If you want to advance in your career, it's important that decision-makers and influencers remember who you are and what makes you unique among all the people that spend time in front of them every day. Show your personality, your sense of humor and your passion.

Do it your way. That's a pretty good description of how an exceptional middle manager shows up at important meetings with senior execs.

Just Because They're Pretty, Doesn't Mean They're Smart

If you thought the title of this section was referring to people, shame on you. We're talking about presentations here! Seriously, when it comes to a slide presentation, there's a real risk that form will overwhelm function—that your slides will be visually impressive, but that there might not be sufficient depth of understanding just below the surface. The software tools we have at our disposal these days make it easy to create a very impressive-looking business presentation. We have all seen our share of presentations that look more like high-priced advertising campaigns but are actually talking about mundane business issues.

In fact, for a period of time in my career, I worked in a division where everyone was required to apply an extensive list of graphic standards – font, color, images, etc. — to our internal presentations, to make them look as much as possible like the advertising and marketing content that was being presented to the public via print ads, TV ads, and web-based content.

While it's true, as one of my outplacement counselors told me, "Don't kid yourself, in business we are always marketing to each other in every conversation.," it's also true that you should be careful to not get carried away with the design aspect at the expense of the content of your presentation.

A few years ago, I was in a frank discussion with some colleagues from all over the world. One of the UK attendees had the courage to tell me that he thought Americans appeared to be overly comfortable with a superficial understanding of a topic, while Europeans required more depth of understanding. He said, "You guys seem to think five bullets on a slide are all you need, and you look down at us if we start asking for more information before we're ready to jump on the bandwagon and share your passion. You need to understand that we're not disagreeing with you, we just believe in doing our analysis before coming to a conclusion." (He also found it curious that Americans talked so much about "passion" when it came to business.)

It's also worth noting that Jeff Bezos banned the use of PowerPoint from internal meetings at Amazon, calling it the "smartest thing we ever did."[14] Instead of slide presentations, Amazon requires the presenter to prepare a "six-page, narratively-structured memo" and the meeting begins silently, with each attendee reading that memo before discussing the topic.[15]

The critical point that I'd like you to take away from this section is this: it doesn't matter whether you are communicating your information to your execs via slides, six-page memos, or two-minute elevator speeches. The key thing is that before you open your mouth and put yourself out there, you know what you're talking about, you have a clear objective, and you are prepared to respond effectively to any question that might come up.

Before we leave this topic of exec presentations, I'd like to share a few more of my own personal rules with you:

→ Always assume that any meeting scheduled with an exec has a 50/50 chance of being canceled or rescheduled. Don't take it personally, and don't read any meaning into it. Execs are busy people. You are not likely their highest priority, and odds are that an assistant changed the schedule, and the exec may not know that, or may not even know that they had a meeting with you in the first place.

→ When you're trying to reach someone to set up a meeting, exec or otherwise, and you're getting no response to email or text messages, try sending them a meeting request instead. Some people get way more email on a daily basis than they can ever read. I once asked a very senior exec how he managed wading through hundreds of emails every day. He responded that he actually opened emails only from people he knew and assumed that if other messages were important, they'd eventually get his attention.

I realized that any email I sent to an exec could be easily go unnoticed, but if I sent a meeting request for a specific date, then that invite would show up in their calendar and they, or the person who managed their calendar, would likely see it and have to deal with it somehow. And that might give me the opportunity to explain why I was requesting a meeting.

→ And, speaking of the people who provide direct support to your execs —whether they are called executive assistants, admins, secretaries, or whatever – they can be of enormous value to you. When you want access to the exec, it is almost always smart to contact their assistant, explain your request, and enlist their support. The assistant not only knows the exec and the exec's schedule better than anyone else, they can also be of great value in educating you on the finer points of connecting and working effectively with their boss. Assistants keep the executive trains running on a daily basis, and you should strive to know as many of them as you can. That simple approach is definitely on the path to achieving strategic advantage in the workplace.

That's the end of our discussion on how to deliver effective presentations to executives. Whether you have succeeded famously in this regard or failed miserably, this might be a good time to discuss how to land that next job.

PART 3
HOW TO ADVANCE YOUR CAREER IN TODAY'S JOB MARKET

CHAPTER 9
A SMARTER WAY TO THINK ABOUT CAREER PROGRESSION

To kick off this section, I want to mention that at two important junctions in my career, I was given the opportunity to accept a generous severance package or another job—and both times I took the money. Both packages included some "outplacement" career counseling with some top people in that field, and I came away with invaluable insights that I will be sharing with you later in this section.

At the same time, however, I have to admit that when I'm in career coaching mode, I often refer back even further in time to some of the most basic reference tools I discovered in the early stages of my career. Simple truths never go out of style, and I'll also be sharing some of those with you in this section.

Job hunting is another area where numerous books, blogs, articles, seminars etc. can be found at any time, all promising to endow you with some kind of special advantage so that you can blow past everyone else and achieve your dream career. Most of these publications and programs repackage the same old guidelines, but regardless of what model you find the most interesting, it's worthwhile to focus on some clear, memorable, and enduring principles. The first of these have to do with how you know when it's time for a career change.

If the Job Fits…

There is probably not one person reading this who has not at one time or another—possibly at this very moment—wondered if it was time to look for another gig. There are many reasons we might arrive at this point, and I've been there several times myself.

Long ago, when I was struggling to decide whether it was time to leave the banking industry and find a more satisfying career path, I would go to the Seattle library on my lunch hours and pour through all the career guidance books that were in print at that time. I don't remember the names of all the books or the specific guidance I encountered back then, but I came away from that exercise with this enduring conclusion: you know it's time to change jobs when the "fit" just isn't right anymore.

If you're already a middle manager or leader in your organization, hopefully you accepted the job that you're in because it seemed like a good fit for you at the time. But as time goes by in the real world, conditions change, companies change, your needs change, and sometimes the job just doesn't feel right anymore. You may feel the need to make a move when there are changes in your management or when your company gets acquired or downsizes. Or perhaps *you* have changed in some way, e.g., you've developed new skills, or you've simply become bored or unhappy with a job that, at one time, may have met your needs but no longer does.

And here's a critical point that you will rarely see in any of those top selling career guides: there are few things that will make an employee more miserable in their job than having a manager who, for any reason, causes you relentless pain, fear, discomfort, or uncertainty. You may work for a great company with great benefits and everything you thought you wanted, but if the fit with your manager isn't right, that is very often a strong signal that it's time to change jobs. One of the top executives I've admired used to say that since he was a young boy his father told him, "Don't live with pain." That seems like very good advice to apply to your personal career planning. *Be your own agent* and strive to achieve the best outcomes you can for your most important client: *you.*

Of course, many of us are creatures of habit, and the idea of stepping out of our current comfort zone, even if it's to leave an unsatisfactory work situation, can be challenging. A common dilemma when the job fit isn't good is in trying to decide whether it's best to pursue a new career path in a different organization, or to stay put and try harder in hopes of advancing up through the organization you're in. So, let's spend some time talking about when and why it is, or isn't, time to go ahead and make a career move.

Nobody Knows You Like You Do

That may seem like a clever, catchy title for this topic, but I'd really like you to take a moment to consider this: it is highly unlikely that there is anyone on this planet—your best friend, your parents, your mate, etc.—who truly knows how you're thinking and feeling at all times. It's a fact of life that each of us has to adjust our behavior, enhance our appearance, and manage our speech much of the time in order to interact effectively with the people around us. This is true in all interpersonal encounters, but it's especially true in your work life, where you might have to "go along to get along."

Only you know how you feel as you're heading home at the end of a workday. Was it uncomfortable? Uplifting? Boring? Annoying? Inspiring? Even when someone you care for asks, "How are you doing?" or "How was your day?" only you know whether the answer you give is true and complete.

The point is this: if you want to have a truly satisfying career, then you need to be honest with yourself about what is truly satisfying for you. Too often, when we're first starting out and looking at what we perceive to be the career path ahead of us, we think in terms of titles and levels, rather than how we want to spend the major portion of our lives that we will dedicate to work. It's so common to hear something like "In five years, I want to be at this level" rather than "For me to have a fulfilling career, I need to spend my time doing x."

Many of us have grown up believing our working life is a competitive proposition where the ultimate goal is status, title, and even some form of dominance over other people. There may have been specific activities in your life—sports for example—where these things really were the objective. However, when it comes to your career, where you are working in collaboration with other people in pursuit of a common goal, the pursuit of status rather than personal fulfillment can be a huge mistake. It can result in a lifetime of stress, disillusionment, and disappointment for you and for the people whose lives you have impacted along the way. My advice:

Make the effort to figure out who you really are and then *be your own agent* and find the right job for that person.

One book that helped me get more focused on the key elements of job satisfaction was Barbara Sher's *Wishcraft*, which was on the job-hunting best seller list way back in the late '70s and is still in print today. I did not subscribe to every phase of the step-by-step plan she laid out in that book, but I did extract one very special principle: after you determine who you really are and what accomplishments are the most satisfying for you, then you should envision a job that embodies those elements and go find that job.

A useful illustration, one that I've employed in many career coaching situations, is a person who says, "I really want to be a doctor." In essence, they are citing a job title, and on the surface it's not actually clear what they are envisioning they would do in this role, or the benefits they expect. If you were to dig deeper, here are some of the possible responses that you might hear:

→ "Doctors have a lot of status in our society and make a lot of money. I want status and money. I can see myself as a celebrity plastic surgeon in Beverly Hills."

→ "Doctors help people who are suffering. I get a lot of satisfaction out of helping people. I can see myself working in an inner-city clinic, or maybe even overseas with Doctors Without Borders."

→ "Doctors have to master a lot of science, and I love molecular biology. I can see myself working as a research scientist in a lab, helping to solve the top medical mysteries of our era."

Once you learn to avoid aiming at a job *title* as your career objective, and focus instead on the *functions* that you will perform, you may discover that there are any number of roles in which you can perform those functions and find job satisfaction. But you'll only get there if you are honest with yourself about what works and doesn't work for you. And then, as I'll point out below, you need to confirm that any opportunity you're looking at really is what you think it is.

When you're trying to define your target position, a useful technique is to create a worksheet where you identify and prioritize the attributes of a job that matter more for you. Your list might contain items like these:

- → Title
- → Money
- → Location
- → Diversity of workforce
- → Work-at-home option
- → Length of commute
- → Travel opportunities
- → Company Culture
- → Service to Humanity
- → Growth Opportunity
- → Training Opportunity

Build yourself a scoresheet in which you identify the factors that matter to you, then assign a numeric weighting—perhaps 0-3—for each factor to indicate its relative importance. Later, when you are applying for specific openings, you can assign a score for each factor for each of the positions you're considering and multiply by the weighting number to get a final tally by job opportunity. You may find the process illuminating.

I went through this exercise as I was transitioning from the banking sector to the tech sector. I was surprised to discover that, after many years of working in the city, the hours spent commuting, along with high-priced parking, had become a bigger issue for me than I realized. When I decided that I simply didn't want that long commute anymore, I placed high importance on finding a job where my home and my office were closer together, preferably both on the same side of the lake that I had been driving across for all those years. And it worked; every job I've had since then has met these criteria. For the last 20 years of my working life, my commute was never more than about 15 minutes, and I counted my blessings every day. Think about what will make you count your blessings, then *be your own agent* and search for those variables in the positions you're considering.

Thinking About a Career Change—but Today Is Not a Good Day…

One type of thinking I've encountered many times goes like this: "I really want to work in that career path over there, but I'm going to stick it out here for a while longer in order to build skills, improve my resume, etc. so that I'll be more attractive to that other organization." Admittedly, there are times when this strategy makes sense, e.g., when your current organization can help you to obtain the credentials needed to get into that other organization.

But too often I've seen this same logic applied when it's really nothing other than simple procrastination or reluctance to change. Often this reluctance evolves into to an inability to take action, leading to serious disappointment, especially when it starts with young people early in their careers. I've known more than a few twenty-somethings who thought they were just going to log a short time in their current job before they finally crossed over into something they really wanted to do, and I've watched several of those people arrive in their 40s, doing the same job and wondering where all the time had gone.

When we're just starting out, it often seems like there will be plenty of time to make job-related changes later. What many people don't realize at that early stage is that once you've settled into a job situation, things have a way of slowing down as your commitments increase.

When you're young and free and unencumbered and socially active, it's easy to assume you can always change your mind and your circumstances any time you want. But as many of us have learned, as time passes and you take on the constraints that accompany personal relationships, housing commitments, debt, family, etc., your flexibility can be greatly reduced. And that's just part of the reason that procrastination is a bad strategy.

A far more important reason is that the longer you stay in your current position, the less interesting you may appear to be to the organization you really want to work for. While you've been building that successful record in your current role, what you think of as assets may actually be liabilities. You may have moved up in job level and increased your salary such that there are fewer positions available in that other org that will fit your current requirements. You may see yourself as a proven high achiever, while they may view you as too expensive to bring in as a trainee in their space. Also, the longer you're achieving success in your current role, the more you start to look like you belong there.

At about the same time that I embraced the concept of job fit, and decided I was ready for a career change, I made a few attempts to apply for other positions in the bank I worked for. I had achieved a certain amount of success in my current division—promotions, salary increases, etc.—and I expected to be an attractive candidate to other groups. I was confused when they didn't show sufficient interest, and (being my own agent) I took the courageous step of going to the head of HR to ask what I must be missing.

His response was enlightening. First, he was surprised that I was interested in these other roles, then he said, "Well, let's talk about 'the book' on you." He proceeded to tell me how I was perceived in the company, essentially as a rising star in the group that I was already in, and how other departments within the company might have a difficult time envisioning me in their world, especially when compared to qualified candidates who they already knew and admired in their own organization.

Over time, as I became a hiring manager myself, I recognized the truth of this message, and I came to this conclusion: if there is a career path you know you want to pursue, get on it as soon as possible. The sooner you cross over to that path—even if you have to accept a lesser role than you hoped for—the easier it will be to find a position you can fit into, and the sooner you will start learning that business and developing your value in the world you want to be in. Don't wait until you think you'll have more trading power. Go there now, take the best job you can get, and start growing up in that organization, where *you* can now become that candidate with the inside strategic advantage.

Where's the Money?

Another self-defeating tendency I've observed, especially in younger, high-achieving employees, is the belief that if they stay where they are—where they are valued—they will continue to receive all the rewards they deserve. This belief is often based on the fact they've already received rapid promotions and rewards in a short period of time; they feel like a winner in the current organization, and they expect that to continue. Well, here are two more lessons that you may learn after you've been on the job for a while:

→ If you're talented, it only makes sense that you will move up relatively quickly in the early stages of your career. Don't make the mistake of thinking that if you've earned X promotions in your initial few months or years, you're going to continue at that blistering pace.

→ In large hierarchical organizations, the number of positions and levels you can aspire to typically gets smaller as you move up the organization. The higher you go, the fewer opportunities there are to go higher, and the greater the competition for that dwindling number of opportunities.

Unless you are in a role where you can drive your compensation up via commissions and bonuses, I believe that the fastest way to significantly increase your salary is via promotion, not by waiting for annual merit increases to get you there. The advantage of promotions over merit increases is often a difference of double-digit vs. single-digit increases, plus you may actually have more ability to influence the frequency of promotional increases than you do to influence merit increases, bonuses, or other forms of compensation.

It's important to note, however, that there are times when a promotion can turn out to be something different than what you expected. It's very important to make sure you know what you are pursuing, including whether the actual salary and compensation will be what you expected, from day one. Let's talk a little about the potential risk…

It seems to me that some companies have lost their way when it comes to how their compensation systems are structured. In my view, the level and salary of a job should be based on the skills required to do that job, along with the competitive market value associated with that role. This is a standard methodology that HR professionals have employed for many years, and many companies might argue that this is exactly the model they follow—even when they don't.

Sometimes if you carefully analyze the rules regarding promotion, you may discover two conflicting approaches existing side-by-side. For example, the official promotion rules might appear to be based on the principle that there is an appropriate level and salary for each role, and that when an employee (or candidate) is qualified, they should move to that level and salary. But in real practice, even when a high-performing employee is clearly deserving of a promotion, there is often an elaborate explanation for why a promotion is not possible at this time, or perhaps that you can receive the promotion in title, but for some reason now is not the right time to pay you the corresponding salary.

For a variety of reasons, mostly related to how corporate compensation programs can become over-designed, and over-constrained, you may encounter this commonly-heard— and often valid—complaint: someone coming into an organization from the outside can often start at a higher salary than a proven employee who is already there and doing a good job. Rather than complain about the unfairness of that situation, however, I suggest you take advantage of it. Become your own agent, and start figuring out where your next promotion is coming from. And if your current management can't answer that question, you may have just discovered that the job fit isn't good anymore and it's time to move on.

I like to think of promotions as existing in two dimensions: *internal* and *external*.

An *internal* promotion involves moving up within your current organization. While this is a positive sign that your management values you and your contribution, it can also paradoxically introduce some "drag" in your career progression. Some organizations have policies about how frequently a person can be promoted, or when promotions can be granted. So, regardless of your performance and the pace at which you're developing, you may be put in an arbitrary holding pattern because you were recently promoted or the next scheduled promotion cycle is months away. And, if your company, in an ill-conceived attempt to control salary expense, puts a limit on the number of promotions that will be allowed in your group within a certain time period—a really stupid, but all-too-familiar concept—then your "turn" may not come around again for a long time.

I've also seen scenarios in which, rather than moving you to the established level and salary for the new position, management may be more inclined to look at your previous compensation level and give you a modest, below-market increase, sometimes justifying that with a statement like, "You'll be new at this level; let's go slow and give you a chance to prove yourself."

Things can be even worse if you're in one of those competitive stack-rank systems we talked about in the Performance Assessment discussion. You might even hear the argument that you should actually retain your current job level when you move into the new position, so that you are not at a competitive disadvantage when you get to the new group, i.e., having to compete against people who have been at the higher level for a long time.

Or another favorite: "We're going to give you a small increase now so that there's plenty of room in the salary band to give you another increase in the future." Really? What employee in their right mind wouldn't want all the money they can get now, right up front, even it if meant a smaller increase in the future? Do the math.

In my view, these types of rationalizations are utter B.S. They too often reflect the fact that an organization, in a thinly-veiled attempt to constrain salary expense, has allowed their compensation system to go off the rails, resulting in an approach that is confusing, unfair, and frustrating for everyone involved.

It's an enlightened company in which each job is leveled as it should be and pays the right salary for that level, and where each employee, based on their skills and performance, has a clear opportunity to be in the right job with the corresponding level, title, and salary. It's that simple; why do companies keep screwing it up?

If you find yourself working for a group that can't seem to get this right, you might opt for the second approach. An *external* promotion can take two tracks: to a higher-level position in a different team elsewhere in your company, or to a higher-level position in a different company altogether. Ironically, for some of the same reasons cited above, it's often the case that your own company, where you presumably can offer the most value, is constrained in how much they can offer you, while another company who wants access to those same skills will pay you more upon arrival… after which they may apply similar constraints of their own.

I'm not suggesting that in order to escape these constraints, everyone should jump from job to job and company to company, especially not if you're essentially satisfied where you're at. But if it's money that you're concerned about, and you don't have the ability to influence your own compensation via commissions or incentive-based bonuses, then steering yourself toward a path of relatively frequent promotions may be the best strategy for you.

As you think about job fit, another important factor to consider is how you will be valued and rewarded based on the role that you take on. There is an old adage that "the staff serves the line and the line serves the people." I used to think that was critically important because it seemed to me that front-line jobs in my organization, e.g. front-line sales positions that dealt directly with customers, seemed to be viewed as more important and were more highly rewarded than the rest of us in the staff positions who made it all work *for* the line.

I later developed a more refined view of the principle:

The role you're in might be highly valued in one organization, and of less value in another, depending on how critical it is to the success of the business.

Here's an example: suppose you are a highly skilled IT Pro. In a technical consulting company, you may be the most valuable asset they have. *You* are the product. They will do everything they can to help you succeed, and they will reward you for that success.

In another company where IT is *not* the product—for instance a real estate office or small retail store—a person with the very same skill set, while highly appreciated by everyone who doesn't understand what they do, will not be viewed as a front-line employee and may not be eligible for any of the rewards that the front line enjoys, e.g., promotions, bonuses, commissions, etc. Also, if you're in a supporting role in a business that's focused on something other than your contribution, you may be stuck in a dead-end job with no career path and no choice but to change jobs—or change companies—if you want to advance.

The moral of this story: when you've figured out what you want and need to do for maximum job fulfillment, then consider where that role is valued most—where *you* can be the front-line rock star in the organization—and then point yourself in that direction. This is a key success factor in the *be your own agent* approach.

Peter Almost Got It Right—But Are You Incompetent... or Incompatible?

Back in the day—some 50 years ago!—*The Peter Principle* was a very popular book in which Dr. Laurence J. Peter somewhat satirically asserted that people in a hierarchy tend to rise to their "level of incompetence." In other words, high performing employees continue to be promoted based on their success at each job level, until they attain a job where they do not have the necessary skill to succeed.[16] This is another one of those points that seems so obvious you might wonder how this book sold over a million copies and is still in print today. Yet, if it's so obvious, why do so many managers continue to advance until they've reached their level of incompetence? One likely reason is that we high-achievers tend to assume we can do a good job at anything we apply ourselves to, thinking, "I've always succeeded in the past; why wouldn't I succeed at this too?"

As recently as 2019, a group of researchers—Alan Benson, Danielle Li, and Kelly Shue—published an article in the *Quarterly Journal of Economics*, in which they discussed their efforts to determine whether the Peter Principle is a legitimate, observable phenomenon in business today. In other words, they sought to determine whether organizations are impacted negatively by promoting workers into manager roles based on successful past performance in lower-level jobs, rather than prioritizing whether the candidate demonstrates high potential for performing managerial tasks. Their study was focused specifically on the universe of sales workers who have been promoted into sales management roles. However, their findings are probably valid for many types of roles across the business spectrum.

Here, in their own words, is a summary of their findings:

We use detailed microdata on the performance and promotions of sales workers at a large number of firms to provide the first large-scale test of the Peter Principle, the notion that firms prioritize current performance when making promotion decisions, at the expense of choosing those best suited for the post-promotion role. Consistent with this hypothesis, we find that firms are substantially more likely to promote top salespeople, even when these workers make worse managers on average and on the margin. This behavior results in firms promoting workers who decrease subordinate performance by 30%, relative to a promotion policy that optimizes match quality." [17]

So, it appears that Dr. Peter got it right and gave us a principle that has held up for a half-century! (He clearly had not yet reached his own level of incompetence.)

To be honest, while I've always enjoyed the satirical nature of the Peter Principle, I don't actually believe that high performers are destined to reach their level of incompetence. Some talented people actually do experience success in virtually everything they do and enjoy a long career full of honors and rewards all the way to retirement.

On the other hand, there are occasionally situations in which a very talented person, after a consistent record of high achievement—sometimes dating all the way back to childhood—suddenly finds themselves in the midst of a career crisis. Often, this is the result of having arrived at a level of *incompatibility* rather than incompetence.

Remember: in a hierarchical organization, the higher you go, the fewer opportunities there are ahead of you, the more competition there is for those scarce opportunities, and the more likely it is that some other person may view *their success* as being dependent upon *your failure.* In other words, sometimes very talented people find themselves in a career crisis because they represent a threat to someone else, or even because someone else simply doesn't like them.

It's also possible that you could arrive at your level of incompatibility simply because you pursued a higher-level job for the wrong reasons—status, title, etc.—not recognizing that you were never going to be effective, or happy, in that role.

The takeaway: before you just jump at that next opportunity for a promotion, you should strive to *be your own agent* and think critically about whether you will not only succeed but also be fulfilled in that role. And that brings us to a topic that most of us will visit multiple times over the course of our careers: how to find your next job.

CHAPTER 10
ACHIEVING STRATEGIC ADVANTAGE WHEN APPLYING FOR A JOB

In this section I will talk about several ways that you can *be your own agent* and help yourself to *achieve strategic advantage* as you endeavor to make a career change. These guidelines will benefit you at every stage of your career, from the time you apply for your first job, to any point later in your career when you are evaluating new opportunities or negotiating for a new position. As with so many things, it all starts with who you know…

Networking Your Way to the Front of the Line

A major benefit of achieving strategic advantage in the workplace is that you are perceived as a superior performer, an exceptional middle manager, and a candidate for higher positions. To achieve that level of advantage, you simply must employ one of the most powerful tools at your disposal: networking.

You probably don't need me to tell you that effective networking is an absolutely essential part of your career search. Countless experts in the field have been saying that for a very long time. But for many of us, that guidance might have a similar impact to someone telling you that proper eating habits will lead to better health. Sure, we all know it's true, but it's harder for some of us to take up the habit than it is for others.

One reason why a strong network is more important than ever: in today's job market, you need to be constantly aware that—regardless of how much you think you're a perfect fit for an open job, and regardless of how much you want it—the hiring manager may never even know you exist unless you find a way to make personal contact with that person.

You should envision the space between you and the hiring manager as being occupied by a series of barriers—screening mechanisms that are primarily designed to screen you out, not in. These are often automated "Applicant Tracking Systems" that perform key-word searches on all resumes and pass along only the ones with the highest number of hits. In the digital age, when HR is receiving way more online applications than it can handle, software developers have come to the rescue with sourcing algorithms, filtering algorithms, matching algorithms, and more. These tools not only pre-screen the long list of applicants down to a handful, but also provide HR with a plausible argument that their screening processes are fair and unbiased.

Smaller organizations might still employ a human screener, but whatever form the barrier takes, the goal is to ensure that no more than a few of the hundreds or even thousands of applications received will ever make it to the hiring manager's desk.

In short, if you're going through "normal" channels, e.g., searching for jobs online, submitting your applications, and waiting for a response, you may never hear anything from anybody. And if all you hear is crickets, you shouldn't make the mistake of thinking they read your stuff and decided against you. It could be you simply didn't pass enough barriers in their screening mechanisms, and their system rejected you before anyone even knew you were there.

I will talk a little more below about how to achieve advantage with ATS screening processes, but make no mistake: unless your parents own the company you'd like to work for, there is no more powerful method you can employ to put yourself in front of a hiring manager than reaching out to people who know and support you, and enlisting their aid in helping you to find your next job.

It's important to recognize, however, that networking is not just a matter of telling everybody you know that you're looking for work. In fact, that approach often doesn't work at all. Here are some guidelines to make networking a more powerful tool and a career accelerator for you:

- ➤ Your primary objective in employing your network should be to help you get a face-to-face meeting with the hiring manager for the position you want, or with the person who is managing the recruiting process on behalf of the hiring manager.

- ➤ Whether you see yourself as a salesperson or not, networking is a lot like sales. As your own agent, you have to identify leads, contact those leads, make cold calls if necessary, cultivate those relationships, and stay connected for as long as it takes to achieve your objective. That could be days, weeks, or even months depending on your situation. And, if you're smart, you'll maintain those network connections for the duration of your career.

- ➤ Here's a key point for those who are between jobs: you need to work your network every day as if that *is your job*. Put another way, finding a full-time job can be a full-time job. If you don't take it that seriously—if you just post a couple of applications online, collect your unemployment check, and head for the beach— you may find yourself becoming a less and less desirable, and a less motivated candidate, especially if you've been out of work for a while. And if you're in this category, beware of the common urge to "take some time off" between jobs. It's much better to drive hard on landing that new job, secure the offer, and then take a break simply by setting a start-date that gives you some well-deserved time off.

→ You should not view a personal network as a tactic that you employ only during times of career crisis. If you find yourself reaching out to someone you haven't contacted in ten years, that person is more a previous acquaintance than a member of your network. A vibrant network is something that you develop, grow, and maintain over time. If you believe someone is important to you, then you need to make yourself important to them. Stay in touch. Show an interest in their world and their life. Be a member of *their* network. Be a friend.

→ It's one thing to identify your network; it's another to actually use it. This is another example of "concept vs. execution." It's easy to compile a list of people you know, perhaps consisting of former colleagues, friends, teachers, and others. But it's only when you've reached out to them with a request for support, and they've responded with that support, that you are actually networking. As soon as you've created your list, you need to work your list. As is true of resumes, it's not the document that matters most; it's using it to make connections with people who can help you meet your objectives.

→ However, before you leap into action, there is one more point to cover: you should not reach out to a member of your network until you know specifically what you want to ask for. A network is a valuable personal asset that you don't want to waste. A common but totally ineffective approach would be to blast a message out to everyone you know saying something like, "Hey everybody, I'm looking for a new job. Please let me know if you hear of anything." You will likely get zero responses to a message like that, or even worse, you may get a few suggested options that don't fit you at all.

Before you make initial contact with any member of your network, you should have already gone through the process of deciding what type of role you're looking for and you should spell that out in your message, e.g., "I'm looking for a position as a C++ programming lead in a tech start-up" or "I'd like to find a position as a sales manager with a nationwide retailer" or "I'm hoping to land a financial advisor position in a major banking organization." Now, you've given your network members something very specific to think about. They may already know of a position that fits your description, or they may be able to put you in touch with someone else who does. Additionally, if they encounter anything that sounds even close to what you described in the days ahead, they are much more likely to think of you and help make the connection.

→ Do not wear out your network prematurely. If you keep hitting up the same people over and over again, you may exhaust their goodwill and lose their support, especially if they have extended themselves for you in the past and it didn't yield results. You need to think strategically about what each member of your network brings to the table—the potential value that each person might be able to provide to you, and at what point in the process. One person might be able to introduce you to a key contact in their company; another person might be willing to provide a high-impact letter of recommendation; another person might be a good sounding board to help you refine your communications.

→ You might find that the most helpful person in your network turns out to be someone you hadn't even thought of initially. Here's an example of when my personal network worked particularly well for me. There was an opening in a local company that I found interesting. I tried to figure out how to reach the hiring manager, but I wasn't having much luck. Then I did a search of that company on LinkedIn and discovered that someone I had worked with many years ago—someone who was not on my network list—had worked at the company in the past. They didn't work there anymore, but I reached out anyway and asked if we could get together for coffee so I could learn more about the company and the position. As we talked, she concluded that I would be a good fit for the position in question, and she introduced me to the head of HR, who agreed to meet with me the next day. In essence, I passed up everyone else who was waiting to be screened and went right to the person who could connect me to the hiring manager. That is extreme *strategic advantage*! Within no time, I had interviewed with both of them. While it turned out that I did not get that job—and in retrospect I'm glad I didn't—the LinkedIn networking approach was a total success and a best practice that I've promoted ever since.

How to Pass the Screens

Even with a well-developed network, you may often find yourself in the position of submitting your application into an online process where you don't know anybody and don't have any kind of advantage. It's also important to point out that potential employers could be proactively looking at you when you don't even know it, often via sourcing algorithms that scan LinkedIn and other online recruiting profiles. In both scenarios there are a few important things to remember:

➜ Writing a resume or an online summary of your experience is often hard, and most of us don't enjoy it. Unfortunately, many people tend to short-cut this uncomfortable task, when they should instead be investing a lot of thought and care into the process.

➜ Here's a simple rule: if you know that an automated system is searching for candidates who match specific skills and experience, i.e., who exhibit specific keywords, then by all means make sure those keywords appear, exactly as written in the job posting, in all of your searchable content—resume, cover letter, LinkedIn profile, etc. For those of you wondering if this means that every application must be custom-tailored to each specific opening… absolutely! Remember: you're trying to get as many keyword hits as you can to convince a non-human algorithm to pass you along to the next stage.

➜ Once you succeed in passing the automated screens, then hopefully a human being—possibly another screener, or perhaps a recruiter—will be looking at your information. At this point, it's important that you appear to be not only qualified, but also interesting and compelling. Far too many job searchers kill the buzz by what I think of as a lazy, cut-and-paste approach to resume building. The worst example of this is where each job title and dates of employment are followed by a listing of duties and responsibilities that were clearly copied and pasted right out of some job description. The focus is wrong, the verb tense is wrong, the energy is wrong—it's all wrong. Yet I see it being done all the time, often by highly qualified people. When the screener or hiring manager sees this type of resume, their first impression of you is that you're lazy, unimaginative, and not taking this application or this presentation of your qualifications seriously. In other words, "This person is not trying to impress us… and we're not impressed."

→ A guiding principle of resume writing that has been immortalized is that a resume should highlight a list of accomplishments, not just a list of duties. Yet I see countless examples where people miss this point and only list duties. To be sure, sometimes a job responsibility can embody or imply an important accomplishment or evidence of achievement, e.g., "responsible for a worldwide team of 500 people, a budget of $X million, and sales goals of $Y million." But too often the accomplishments are lost in a boring list of duties.

→ One dead giveaway that you've done little more than copy-and-paste from present and past job descriptions: when duties for past jobs are presented in the present tense—that is, you're implying that you still perform these functions at a company you worked at years ago. I'm amazed how often I see this error, which only sends a loud signal that you didn't take time to think, to edit, or to care about the impression you are making on potential employers. If you're just going through the motions, "phoning it in" on something as important as how you present yourself to potential employers, why should they expect you to perform any better than that if they hired you?

→ These points apply to resume writing but perhaps even more to how you post your career profile on LinkedIn or similar online databases. If you're thinking that you're not actively looking for work but just want to post some information so you have a presence in that forum, you might be tempted to put a minimum amount of effort into it; you might just copy and paste. But, if you seriously hope to advance in your career, you should consider that your next employer— perhaps your ideal employer—could find you online and reach out to you when you're not even thinking about making a career move. In essence, when you post your career profile online, you are auditioning for your next career role. Spend some time reviewing your own profile and those of other people who interest you, or who might be comparable to you or even contenders for the same jobs that you seek. You'll see a lot of sub-standard presentations, and you'll see a few really impressive postings. Bottom line: you can achieve some additional *strategic advantage* just by taking a little more time to optimize your online presentation.

➤ By the way, when you revise your resume to better highlight your accomplishments, remember to express them in a way that triggers those keyword matches, which may be a little different than the language used in the environment you worked in. For example, avoid the use of acronyms that would not be known outside of your company.

Before we leave the topic of how you present yourself on LinkedIn (or in any other social media platform for that matter) I'd like to spend a moment discussing the value of going beyond your profile information and posting additional comments, endorsements, reviews, etc. in an effort to expand your visibility. This is a difficult topic to generalize about, but I would offer this: if you are a highly recognized and respected spokesperson in your field and people are truly interested in what you have to say, then by all means, reach out to your network and share your perspective. But if what you want to post doesn't really help to promote *your* capabilities, *your* skills, *your* expertise, *your* intelligence… don't post it.

In my view, in this era where so many people are striving to develop their personal "brand" and optimize their presence and popularity online, there are too many people posting a whole lot of stuff and making a whole lot of noise that isn't really helping them at all. A good example I see every day are people who incessantly post somebody else's work—articles, videos, books, quotes, etc.—and then "like" or recommend it. I assume they believe that by showing up on the internet every day they are somehow creating visibility, awareness, momentum, and reputation for themselves. But I believe that by pointing only to other people's achievements and never having anything to say about their own, they are actually branding themselves as an observer, a follower, a fan, but not an exceptional middle manager who we would look to for leadership and original thinking. Sure, if you're a wildly popular celebrity, then anything you like or wear or eat might be of intense interest to your followers. But if you're not a celebrity… who cares? Simply put, it's not the number of posts that's important; it's the quality and value of what you are personally *creating*—and then sharing with your audience—that will determine how you are perceived.

We are now at that point where I'd like to call upon some of the thought-provoking things I learned from high-priced "outplacement consultants" when I was moving between companies:

➜ Just like any other market, the job market is in motion out there at all times, whether you're participating in it or not. Jobs are opening and closing daily, but you will likely become aware of them only during the period when you're actively engaged in your job search. In essence, you will have to pick from one of the jobs that's open at the time you're looking... unless you can create your own job.

➜ A good resume is essential, but a resume does not get you a job. The purpose of a resume is to get you an interview, and you should strive to get as many interviews as you can.

➜ The purpose of an interview is to get you a job offer, and you should strive to get as many job offers as you can.

➜ Getting a job offer is not the end of the process; it's the beginning of the next stage of the process. (More on that in a bit).

A consistent but subtle theme in these guidelines is that you should not bet your whole job search on one opportunity. That's especially true because in many instances, you can't know enough about that one position to be certain it's your dream job anyway.

You've likely noticed that I use the phrase "*be your own agent*" throughout this book. As it applies to job hunting, this means getting your client (you) as many job offers as possible and then taking some time to determine which one is the best fit for your client.

There's a phenomenon I've witnessed many times that I'd like to make you aware of now, so that you can watch out for it. It's all about the power of speculation. As we discussed in the "pattern-match" discussion in Chapter 2, it's human nature to try to identify a pattern in a situation where we can't know exactly what's going to happen next, and that happens a lot to people applying for jobs.

When someone doesn't hear back from the hiring company after sending in an application, or perhaps after an interview, many people tend to start attributing feelings or motives to the other party e.g., "They must not like me," "They must have other candidates to talk to," "They must have made an offer to someone else," or similar assumptions. Or, they start inventing arbitrary rules: "If I don't hear back by Friday, that means I didn't get the job." Again, it's normal to try to fill in the blanks, but the risk comes when you convince yourself, in the absence of any evidence, that you must be right, and then you decide to act on that belief. Sometimes people convince themselves that they just can't take it anymore and they just have to take control and do something. And this often results in that person settling for a lesser solution just because it was actionable, not rational.

The fact is, you often don't know what's happening on the other side of the job negotiation, and you don't get to know until someone contacts you. And even though waiting can feel like torture—I've seen job offers come three months after the original interview!—sometimes waiting is exactly what you need to do, rather than taking precipitous action based on scenarios that you actually invented in your own head. I've seen too many people do just that and live to regret it.

One way to avoid the speculation trap is to keep a lot of irons in the fire. In other words, send out multiple applications and line up multiple interviews, so that you are not just sitting and waiting on that one job. For that matter, why would you apply for only one job anyway?

Once we discover what appears to be a desirable position, many of us tend to use our powerful imagination to picture ourselves in that new role, sometimes based on nothing more than a job posting or a job description (which may not even come close to describing the position that's open). Once you've cast yourself in the imaginary role of that new position and envisioned yourself doing whatever you think that job entails, it's pretty easy to get emotionally attached to the picture in your head. And, if you convince yourself that it's the only job for you, then it might seem logical that you wouldn't apply for any other positions, right? Of course, if and when rejection comes, it can be painful, especially when you were positive this was your chosen path.

Again, human nature is a powerful thing, and the best way to avoid that "only-job-for-me" crisis is to follow the experts' advice and make sure you have multiple applications in play at all times. Don't wait for one opportunity to close before you open the next. Put everything in play at once. That way, even if a rejection comes, you can always take heart in the fact that you've got other options in motion and any one of those could be the one.

And, by the way, if you're just *thinking* about a job opening, maybe continuously tweaking your resume or whatever, it's important to recognize that you are not yet in the process of changing jobs, you are not yet a candidate, and in fact you are not actually looking for work. If none of the companies that you're considering as potential employers know you, then you don't exist in their universe. Only when you have delivered your application have you actually applied for a job. That seems so painfully obvious, but it's amazing how many people say they are "looking for a new job" when they actually have not yet taken any action in that direction other than fiddling with their resume. (See the discussion of "concept vs. execution" in Chapter 4.)

And, while we're on the subject of rejection, here's another observation: just because you got turned down doesn't necessarily mean you can't work for that organization. That may sound wrong, but when it comes to job hunting, I've always been something of an optimist and an opportunist, believing the following:

➔ The job description you saw posted somewhere is typically a cut-and-paste compilation that is way overstated. It may or may not describe the role that is actually open, and the hiring manager may or may not absolutely care about every requirement that's stated in the posting, including the college degree or years of experience. In fact, the hiring manager may or may not have even seen the posting before it got posted.

➔ Even if you don't fully meet the requirements, you can still get the job… it happens all the time. You don't have to be the perfect candidate to get hired; you just have to be the best candidate that the hiring manager is aware of at this time.

➔ The more postings there are for the same position, e.g., when a new team is being built, the better your chances of getting one of those positions. If there are seven openings, and you're sixth on the list… you're still in!

➔ Even when you don't get the job you applied for, if you impressed the hiring manager or the recruiters, you still have a shot at getting a different position in the same organization. But you may have to be *your own agent* and drive yourself into that discussion.

➔ There's no harm in trying, and possibly everything to gain.

Here's a personal case in point: shortly after graduating from college, I spent a year banging around Northern California and then decided I should go back to L.A. and find a real job. In those pre-internet days, the typical place to find job postings was in the classified ads section of the local newspaper, in this case the *L.A. Times*. For reasons I no longer remember, an ad for a management trainee position at a major insurance company caught my eye. So, I wrote my cover letter (can't imagine what I had to offer at the time), attached my resume, and sent it in. Next thing I know, I'm interviewing with a number of people at that company. I thought it went very well, but a few days later I was disappointed when they let me know that while they were impressed with me, they gave that job to someone else.

Admittedly, when you get a semi-positive response like that, it's impossible to know whether they really did like you or whether they're just letting you down easy, along with all the other losers. (Who was it that said, "When you come in second, you're actually just the first of the losers"?)

Perhaps it was out of youthful naivete that I thought, "They seem to like me, so what the heck, I'll take another run at them." So, I sent back a letter thanking them for considering me and telling them I was really disappointed because I was very impressed with their organization and was genuinely looking forward to joining their team. And, guess what? I soon got a call from them saying they appreciated my response, they had talked it over amongst themselves, and had decided to create another management trainee position in order to bring me into their company. I had gone from being on top of the list of losers to being the second winner. Never say never.

The Single Most Important Key to a Successful Interview

I have conducted hundreds of interviews during my career, and there's one glaring mistake I've seen over and over again. In a typical interview, someone will ask you about yourself, something like, "Tell me about your work experience" or "Tell me why you're the most qualified person for the job." The absolute worst thing you can do is to launch into what I call "the story of me." I've interviewed candidates who focused exclusively on where they are in their careers, why they need a change, even how they're not getting along with their current manager, or how they don't like the company they work for. In other words, the candidate is focused on *their* needs and how I, the employer, could help them to solve *their* problems.

If you don't learn anything else in this section, learn this: no matter what the interviewer asks you, your answer should go to how you can help the hiring company to solve *their* problems, not yours. You should always assume that the hiring manager has more problems to solve than they can handle and that if you are viewed as the best available candidate to help them solve one or more of those problems, you are likely to get an offer.

You need to do some homework to develop yourself into this kind of compelling candidate. You should prepare for every interview by knowing as much as you can about the company, the group you're applying to, the people you will meet with, and whatever challenges they're facing. Think about the solutions they must be considering. Sometimes there are strong clues in the job posting regarding the gaps they need to fill, the skills they need to acquire, or the new products or programs they are developing. Check them out online; review their own press releases in addition to the stories that have been written about them. Search by the company name on LinkedIn and see if you know any person who works for—or used to work for—that company. Dig in and learn more than they expect you to know when you walk into that interview. After all, in any relationship, nobody is more interesting *to* us than someone who appears to be interested *in* us, right?

Once you have even a partial understanding of their universe—which by itself could put you a lap ahead of most other candidates (strategic advantage)—you should wrap your responses around how you can help them to meet their challenges and solve their problems. Say something like, "I recognize that you're facing a real challenge in transitioning to blah... I think the skills that I developed in my role at XYZ Corp. will enable me to help you get there faster (or at a lower cost, or with fewer bugs, or whatever)." It's a subtle but powerful technique, sometimes so subtle that the manager doesn't know exactly why you stand out from among all the other candidates... somehow you just seem to be a better fit for the team... someone who could plug right in and add value from day one.

Hooray, You Got the Offer, but You're Not Done Yet

When I received the high-priced outplacement counseling I mentioned earlier, I followed the expert's guidance and succeeded in landing a great job offer with a top company. I called my counselor to thank him for all his help and to notify him I wouldn't be meeting with him anymore. His response was, "Wait; don't just accept the offer. You are now at the next step in the process." Thanks to his invaluable coaching, I proceeded to have some additional conversations with the hiring manager, and I was so glad I did.

Remember that whole discussion about how your mind fills in the blanks? It's important to know that, even after your Interview, the hiring manager may have a different understanding of the role than you do. It's possible that the job description you read didn't really describe the role they actually have in mind. It's possible that the words spoken did not mean the same thing to them as they meant to you, and nobody detected that. It's possible that you were so busy trying to impress the interviewer that you missed a phrase somewhere that would have been a red flag if you had heard it. It's critically important that you and the hiring manager both have the same picture in your heads as to what this job entails. Therefore, when the offer arrives, a smart response would be, "Thank you so much for the offer; I am really excited by this opportunity to join your team. Now, before I accept, I want to make sure that we share the same vision for this role. I'd like to describe what I understand the job to be—how I will spend my time at work, what I will be accountable for—and make sure we're on the same page" (or words to that effect).

When I took the outplacement expert's advice, and went back to the hiring manager to clarify the details of the job I had been offered, an interesting thing happened. The manager said, "Oh, I'm glad you brought that up. Since we initially talked to you, we've gone through a reorganization, and the duties of this position have changed somewhat."

My coach had advised me that if there were any surprises, I should take a breath, thank them for the new information, and buy a little more time to think it over. I did just that and returned to the hiring manager's recruiter the next day with a response like this: "I really appreciate the offer, and can't wait to be a member of this team, but after hearing about the new definition of the role, it seems like a bigger job to me, and I'm wondering now if the compensation you offered really fits the job." The recruiter said he'd get back to me, and when he called a few hours later, he said, "Good catch. We agree that it's a bigger job, and we'd like to increase the offer."

That's a great story from a compensation standpoint, but it's even more important from the standpoint of making sure the job you're about to commit yourself to is actually the same as what you were envisioning. Failing to verify this is to risk being confused, disappointed, frustrated, and pinned down in a new job you wish you hadn't taken. It happens all the time; *be your own agent* and don't let it happen to you.

To close this chapter out, I'd like to report that while I was in the midst of writing this book, my daughter earned her PhD and kicked off a job search of her own. Her goals were ambitious; she had very specific requirements for the type of job and the type of organization she wanted to work for. She wanted to move across several states, and she hoped to secure some relocation money and a very substantial salary increase in the process. I'm happy to report that she employed many of the principles outlined in this chapter, and she repeatedly moved to the head of the candidate line with several different organizations. In the end she landed her dream job and she and her employer are delighted with her fit in the new organization.

Hopefully these job-hunting guidelines will help you to land your dream job too. And when you do, I hope this book serves as a handy reference and trusted advisor for all those other challenging situations you are going to encounter in your role as an *exceptional middle manager.*

CLOSING THOUGHTS

One person who read an early draft of this book wondered if the section on job hunting should be at the beginning, because isn't that where a business career begins? I considered that option but decided to open with topics that are probably more immediately relevant to middle management readers who are already in a management role and have current management challenges to address, before they start thinking about their next role.

But, ideally, the order of the chapters in a book like this really shouldn't matter. There's a familiar "rinse and repeat" cycle that most of us follow during our working lives:

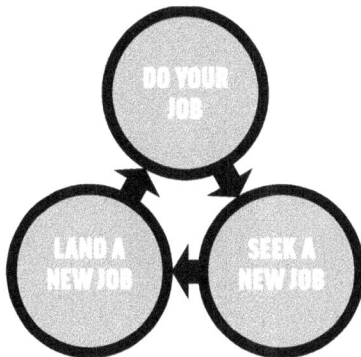

Sure, there are some fortunate people who land the job of their dreams early in life and stick with it for their entire career. Blessed are they.

I envision this book to be more of a reference guide than a linear, instructional program with a finish line. As with any reference book, manual, or handbook, the reader should be able to go directly to the topic that is relevant to their current need, whether it be hiring, managing, communicating, or looking for their next new job. I hope this book works for you in that manner and that you will keep it close at hand.

Each chapter of this book is intended to help you secure the best possible outcomes for your team, for your company, and for yourself as you encounter each of the challenges we've discussed. As I said earlier, being a middle manager can be a solitary experience. Unless you are already a very high-profile, celebrity-level talent, it is unlikely that there is anyone in your world, except you, who is going to be continuously committed to looking out for your best career interests. That is why you must *be your own agent*! Figure out who it is you want to be and what it is you want to do, and then take charge of your career and drive yourself there.

I can assure you that over the course of a long career as a leader and manager, you will encounter many if not all of the scenarios we've discussed here, in whatever order they occur. I hope the insights and advice I've shared with you here will serve you well, serve you often, and help you to *achieve strategic advantage* as an *exceptional middle manager* and advance your career in the direction that you really want to go.

Thank you for joining me in a discussion of the things I learned on my career journey, and I hope these lessons serve you well as you pursue yours.

~Jeff

ACKNOWLEDGEMENTS

F irst and foremost I want to thank my wonderful wife Shannon and amazing daughter Anna for their undying support over all those years while I was working hard to learn the lessons that I'm now trying to teach, and for their continuous encouragement that I pursue my dream of making this book a reality.

Secondly, I want to thank every person who I have ever worked for, or worked with, or who reported to me, in addition to all the clients I have worked with in my consulting and mentoring practices. They are too numerous to call out individually, but they know who they are and they have all helped me to develop the insights that I brought to this book.

Finally, I want to thank the publishing industry professionals who I turned to for help in making this a "real" book. These include, Christine Moore of NY Book Editors, a superior editor and a joy to work with, and John Willig, of Literary Services, Inc, a world-class literary agent and content coach who provided invaluable guidance on how to prepare a book to succeed today's marketplace. Finally, I want to express my extreme appreciation for the incredibly creative book design support I received from George Stevens of G Sharp Design. I highly recommend these professionals to any other authors who are looking for highly-talented and trustworthy partners.

ENDNOTES

1   *The Real Value of Middle Managers* by Zahira Jaser, Harvard
    Business Review website, https://hbr.org/2021/06/
    the-real-value-of-middle-managers

2   Doran, G.T. (1981) There's a S.M.A.R.T. Way to Write
    Management's Goals and Objectives. Management
    Review, 70, 35-36

3   *The Little Prince*, Antoine de Saint-Exupéry,
    Harcourt, Inc., 1943

4   *Alice's Adventures in Wonderland*, Lewis Carroll, Macmillan
    & Co., 1865.

5   *How to Create a Mind*, by Ray Kurzweil. Penguin Books
    2013, quoted by QuickRead Summary of *How to Create
    a Mind* by Ray Kurzweil, Free Audio book, https://www.
    youtube.com/watch?v=043S0FSjZ0A [video]

6   *The Psychology of Science: A Reconnaissance* by
    Maslow, Abraham Harold (1966). . Harper &
    Row. ISBN 978-0-8092-6130-7, cited in Wikipedia
    article *Law of the Instrument* https://en.wikipedia.org/wiki/
    Law_of_the_instrument

7   *Ray Kurzweil at DEMOfall 2012*, by IDG TECHtalk,
    October 3, 2012, https://www.youtube.com/
    watch?v=90fznHTXLrI [video]

8   *Management of Organizational Behavior – Utilizing Human Resources* by Hersey, P. and Blanchard, K. H. (1969), New Jersey/Prentice Hall.

9   *Exclusive: Meta slashes hiring plans, girds for "fierce" headwinds,* by Katie Paul, Reuters. com https://www.reuters.com/technology/ exclusive-meta-girds-fierce-headwinds-slower-growth-second-half-memo-2022-06-30/

10   *Google CEO tells employees productivity and focus must improve, launches 'Simplicity Sprint' to gather employee feedback on efficiency* by Jennier Elias, July 31, 2022, CNBC.com, https://www.cnbc.com/2022/07/31/ google-ceo-to-employees-productivity-and-focus-must-improve.html

11   *Elon Musk went on a firing frenzy at Twitter. Now he's paying for it,* by Robert Reich, The Guardian.com, November 21,2022 , https://www.theguardian.com/ commentisfree/2022/nov/21/elon-musk-went-on-a-firing-frenzy-at-twitter-now-hes-paying-for-it?CMP=oth_b -aplnews_d-1

12   *Business as UnUsual,* is a change management training course offered by Pritchett, LP, https://www.pritchettnet. com/change-management-training/business-as-unusual

13   *The Great Attrition is making hiring harder. Are you searching the right talent pools?,* by Aaronn De Smet, Bonnie Dowling, Bryan Hancock, and Bill Schan-inger, McKinsey Quarterly, July 13, 2022, McKinsey & Company website, https://www.mckinsey.com/

capabilities/people-and-organizational-performance/
our-insights/the-great-attrition-is-making-hiring-
harder-are-you-searching-the-right-talent-pools

14   *Jeff Bezos: This is the 'smartest thing we ever did' at Amazon,* as
quoted by Taylor Locke, CNBC.com, October 14, 2019,
https://www.cnbc.com/2019/10/14/jeff-bezos-this-
is-the-smartest-thing-we-ever-did-at-amazon.html

15   *Why Jeff Bezos makes Amazon execs read 6-page memos
at the start of each meeting,* as quoted by Ruth Umoh,
CNBC.com, April 23, 2018, https://www.cnbc.
com/2018/04/23/what-jeff-bezos-learned-from-requiring-
6-page-memos-at-amazon.html

16   *The Peter Principle,* by Dr Laurence Peter and Raymond
Hull, William Morrow and Company, 1969

17   *Promotions and the Peter Principle,* by Alan Benson, Danielle
Li, and Kelly Shue, The Quarterly Journal of Economics,
Volume 134, Issue 4, November 2019, Pages 2085–2134, as
reported at https://doi.org/10.1093/qje/qjz022

CONNECT WITH JEFF!

To learn more about Jeff...
...inquire about personal mentoring services, or buy bulk copies of the book for your company or organization, scan the QR code below or visit https://www.jefflyonmentor.com

To contact Jeff directly...
...email him at jeffllyon@outlook.com or connect with him on LinkedIn at https://www.linkedin.com/in/jllyon/

www.ingramcontent.com/pod-product-compliance
Lightning Source LLC
Chambersburg PA
CBHW040919210326
41597CB00030B/5132